Human Action

Glenn Langford is presently lecturer in philosophy at the University of Exeter, England. He is the author of *Philosophy and Education*.

PROBLEMS IN PHILOSOPHY

◆

Human Action

GLENN LANGFORD

Anchor Books
DOUBLEDAY & COMPANY, INC.
GARDEN CITY, NEW YORK
1971

The Anchor Books edition is the first publication
of *Human Action*
Anchor Books edition: 1971

To David, Juliet, and Sally

Acknowledgments

This book relies heavily on the work of others, especially those whose work is described and discussed, and I would like to acknowledge my debt to them, in particular Professors D. W. Hamlyn and R. S. Peters, both of whom taught me at Birkbeck College. I also wish to express a special debt to Professor D. J. O'Connor for his help, encouragement, and detailed comments, and to thank Mrs. Peggy Martin and Miss Ruth Yendell for typing the manuscript.

TABLE OF CONTENTS

Human Action

CHAPTER I

Introduction

1. *Actions and Events*

Both the death of Caesar and the murder of Caesar by Brutus were events that occurred in Rome during 44 B.C.; but only the latter was an action. Actions therefore are events, though not all events are actions. I will try to say something about the difference between actions and events that are not actions.

Of an event, such as a landslide, we can ask both when and where it happened. We need not witness an event to know that it has taken place; if the road that was clear the previous day is now blocked by rocks we assume that there has been a landslide. Reports of events, therefore, are reports of changes; what has changed in this case is that rocks that were previously littered about the hillside now block the road. Rocks themselves are not events but things. Things, however, change, and it is their changing that constitutes events. The contrast between things and events is obscured by the fact that we often use expressions that are grammatically similar to refer to both. Thus "landslide," "cloudburst," and "sunset" are used to refer to events; "rocks," "cloud," and "sun" refer to things. A further distinction might be made between things and stuffs such as water, earth, and sunlight; here I will include stuffs with things. The most obvious sort of change that occurs to things is changes in their spatial location; what happened when the landslide occurred was that the position of the rocks changed.

Events don't *just* happen. We can usually relate the occurrence of an event to the occurrence of some prior event that caused it to happen. There may, for example, have been prolonged heavy rain during the previous night. We might say that the landslide was caused by the rain, but strictly speaking this would not be correct. Rather it was caused by the rain falling on the hillside, that is, by the rainfall. To point to a cause is not to point to a thing (using the word "thing" to include stuff like water), but to a prior event. The water that was suspended in clouds above the mountain condensed into drops, which fell on it. Though events themselves do not change, they produce or cause change, one change following another in a complex sequence. Any particular event in the sequence may be regarded either as a cause of further change or the effect of prior change, depending on the explanatory context. It is to some extent arbitrary when we say that one event ends and another begins. A billiards cue, for example, moves and hits a ball, which in turn moves and hits others; as a result the position of the balls on the table is changed. The change in the position of the billiards cue, therefore, is an event that may or may not be followed by other events; at least there may be no consequences that we can detect, or none in which we are interested.

Suppose now that the cue, as is likely, is held by a billiards player. The ball moves because it is hit by the cue; and the cue moves because the arm of the man holding it moves. There is a sequence of three events: the movement of the arm causing the movement of the cue, and the movement of the cue causing the movement of the ball. The first event was the movement of a human body; therefore, of the three, it is the most obvious candidate for the status of an action rather than that of a mere physical event, for it is at least clear that actions have something to do with people. But the difference between an action and a physical event cannot just be that what changes in an action is the position of a human body. If this were so it would be difficult to see why we attach the importance we do to those events that are actions; no important contrast between actions and other events would have been made. I will consider therefore a principal reason for making that distinction.

2. *Actions and Responsibility*

An action that consisted only in the movement of an arm, even if accepted *as* an action, would not be thought important. But when Brutus moved his arm on the Ides of March it held a dagger, and the movement of his arm caused the dagger to enter Caesar's body. The movement of his arm was part of a sequence of events that included the movement of the dagger and the death of Caesar. He was therefore regarded as responsible, with others, for Caesar's death. One context, then, in which it is important to pick out actions is that in which questions of responsibility arise.

There is, however, an ambiguity in the word "responsible" between what I will call morally responsible and causally responsible. People are held morally responsible for their actions and the consequences of their actions; in this sense responsible means morally or legally accountable and, therefore, an appropriate subject of praise and blame or punishment. Brutus was certainly responsible for Caesar's death in this sense. In an alternative use of the word "responsible" we say, for example, that prolonged, heavy rain was responsible for the landslide; that is, the heavy rain *caused* the landslide. Similarly, we also say that Brutus was responsible for Caesar's death; that is, Brutus caused Caesar's death. Thus Brutus was responsible for Caesar's death in both senses of the word. Indeed, the question of whether Brutus was morally responsible for Caesar's death would normally arise only after it had been established that he was causally responsible for it. For this reason the subject of action is of central importance for moral philosophy and the philosophy of law. But to say that Brutus was causally responsible is not itself to say that he was morally responsible; what he was morally responsible *for* was causing Caesar's death. What primarily requires elucidation, therefore, is the sense in which Brutus was causally responsible for Caesar's death; and this elucidation cannot be provided in terms of the notion of moral responsibility that presupposes it.

The notion of causal responsibility is, however, itself ambiguous. We say both that Brutus was responsible for (that is, caused) Caesar's death, and that the prolonged heavy rain caused (was responsible for) the landslide. But no matter how many people were killed by the landslide, we would not go on to raise further questions about the moral responsibility of the rain, though we do raise them in the case of Brutus. This suggests that the rain was not causally responsible for the landslide in the same way as Brutus was causally responsible for Caesar's death. Indeed, in certain circumstances we would not hold Brutus morally responsible for Caesar's death, even though Caesar's death was the end of a sequence of events that included the movement of a dagger caused by a prior movement of Brutus' arm. Brutus may, for example, have been showing the dagger to Caesar when they were campaigning in the hills, and the movement of his arm, and therefore of the dagger, may have been caused by a falling rock. In fact, however, when Brutus stabbed Caesar nothing, at least on the face of it, caused his arm to move. But we do not therefore conclude that his arm just *happened* to move; we think that, in Aristotle's words, "the movement of the limbs instrumental to the action originated in the agent himself."[1] We suppose, that is, not merely that nothing external to Brutus' body acted on it to cause it to move in the way that it did, but that Brutus himself was responsible for the movement. His arm moved because he *moved* his arm; he initiated the sequence of events that ended in Caesar's death and was therefore responsible for it. There is, then, an ambiguity in the notion of causal responsibility between the sense in which Brutus was responsible, as agent, for Caesar's death, and the sense in which the heavy rain was responsible, as cause, for the landslide.

Though the two senses of responsibility share the idea of "bringing about"—Brutus brought about Caesar's death and the heavy rain brought about the landslide—they are nevertheless radically different. I pointed out earlier that, strictly speaking, we should say that the landslide was caused not by the rain (a thing or stuff) but by the rainfall (an event), since only events, not things, can occupy the role of causes. If "Brutus was responsible for Caesar's death" is to be understood in the same way as "the prolonged heavy rain caused the landslide," it should be possible and, strictly speaking, even necessary to replace the word "Brutus" with the description of an event. But though possible, it is certainly not necessary to do so in order to express more accurately what we ordinarily want to say. Indeed, to make such a substitution would be to depart from the way we ordinarily speak. There may be reasons for doing so; but, if so, they are metaphysical reasons. We are not obliged to do so in the interests of clarity. For, mistakenly or not, when we say that Brutus killed Caesar we mean that *Brutus* killed Caesar; we are not, that is, using the word "Brutus" to

[1] Aristotle, *The Ethics of Aristotle—The Nichomachean Ethics,* p. 78.

refer to an event as we might use the word "rain" to refer to the rainfall. By "Brutus" we mean the person called Brutus; and persons, though they are not merely things, are not events either. In the next two chapters I will look at accounts of action according to which it is possible to replace "Brutus" in "Brutus killed Caesar" by a description of a physical or mental event. If what I have said is correct, such accounts cannot be wholly successful. In the following chapter, therefore, I will return to the connection between actions and those who perform them.

CHAPTER II

Action and Acts of Will

1. Persons as Bodies and Persons as Minds

I said in the previous chapter that it was not possible, in "Brutus was responsible for Caesar's death," to replace "Brutus" with a description of an event without departing from our ordinary way of speaking. But if Brutus is identified either with his body or with his mind, perhaps this substitution can be made after all. From one philosophical point of view, only material bodies and the relations between them really exist. To speak of Brutus therefore is really to speak of a physical body—the one we normally call Brutus' body. It is then both possible and, in the interest of clarity, desirable to replace "Brutus" with a description of an event, the most likely substitution being a description of a movement of Brutus' body. For the dagger moved because Brutus' arm moved; and Caesar died because the dagger moved and entered his body. In this view, an action is a movement of a human body, i.e., a bodily movement, though we would ordinarily include within the description of the action a reference to its immediate consequences. Indeed, we would often refer to the action by referring to its consequences, as when we say that Brutus killed Caesar.

According to an alternative view, what exists includes both physical bodies (including those of animals and men) and minds; and persons are thought of primarily as minds. Descartes, for example, says in his fourth Discourse on Method that "the mind by which I am what I am, is wholly distinct from the body."[1] Brutus is then identified not with his body but with his mind; and his mind is thought of as the locus of a succession of conscious or mental states or events. And the reference to Brutus in "Brutus killed Caesar" can be eliminated in favor of a description not of a physical but of a mental event. Caesar died because the dagger moved and entered his body; the dagger moved because Brutus' arm moved; and Brutus' arm moved because a mental event occurred in Brutus' mind.

In this chapter I will consider a view of action that presupposes the second of these alternatives, the view that what we ordinarily call an action is a bodily movement caused by a prior mental event. And I will look in some detail at one recent exponent of it.

2. *Prichard's Account of Action*

In "Duty and Ignorance of Fact,"[2] H. A. Prichard argued that to do an action is "to perform a mental activity of a special kind," that of "setting ourselves to do something, i.e.,

---

[1] Descartes, *Discourse on Method*, p. 27.
[2] Prichard. *Duty and Ignorance of Fact* was the Henriette Hertz Lecture for 1932 (Proceeding of the British Academy, 1932): *Acting, Willing, Desiring* is reprinted in A. R. White, *The Philosophy of Action*.

to bring something about."[3] In "Acting, Willing, Desiring," also, his view is that "an action, i.e., a human action, is an activity of willing some change, this usually causing some change, and in some cases a physical change," though it may not do so.[4] This, so far as I can see, is substantially the same view as in "Duty and Ignorance of Fact," though now the phrase "setting oneself to cause" is rejected in favor of "willing." Both however are technical expressions. We do occasionally use similar expressions in nonphilosophical contexts; for example, we might say that someone is setting out to cause mischief, or that an effort of will is needed when getting up on a cold morning. But Prichard's interest is in the "common character"[5] that all actions share; it is not confined to this limited range of cases. Neither expression therefore is self-explanatory, even if capable of explanation, and unless a clear meaning is attached to them a discussion of Prichard's views is bound to be confusing if not vacuous. I will therefore consider the arguments that led him to define action in terms of these expressions, and at the same time try to find out how he intended them to be understood.

In both articles Prichard begins with a view of action that he ultimately rejects, the view that "we mean by 'an action' or 'doing something' . . . originating, causing, or bringing about the existence of something, viz. some new state of an existing thing or substance, or more shortly, causing a change of state of some existing thing." For example, "by 'moving our hand' we mean causing a change of place of our hand; by 'posting a letter' we mean bringing about that a letter is in a pillar-box."[6] In short, to do an action is to bring about or cause change. It is clear that, though rejecting it, Prichard finds this account of action plausible and his own account is based on it and reached through criticism of it.

But, Prichard adds, "we ordinarily think that in doing certain actions we bring about the things which we do directly, while in doing certain others we do so indirectly, i.e., by directly bringing about other things which in turn cause them."[7] Examples of originating something indirectly are "curing our toothache by swallowing some aspirin, and killing another by pressing a switch which exploded a charge underneath him."[8] "Moving or turning our hand" is used as an example of directly causing some new state, though he says that what we really originated directly in such cases "must have been some new state or states of our nerve cells."[9] But what is important for his argument is the fact that we do bring about some changes directly; and this, he thinks, is established once we admit that we bring about some things indirectly. For, he says, "so long as we think that we bring about certain things indirectly, we inevitably imply that there are certain things which we bring about directly, even if we do not know what they are. It is as impossible for all bringing about to be indirect as for all knowledge to be indirect." And only bringing about directly is action in the strict sense; "for, where we bring about something by causing something to cause it, the result is not wholly due to us; . . . in the strict sense of 'action,' our action must cease with the cessation of our activity."[10]

It is clear that a distinction can be made between doing something directly and doing something indirectly. If curing my toothache is something I do indirectly, then there must have been something, such as taking aspirin, that I did directly, since "indirectly" is a relational word requiring a second term. It does not follow that taking aspirin, as such, has a property of directness independent of its relation to curing my toothache. So far as this argument goes, therefore, there need not be any actions that are direct

---

[7] *Ibid.*
[8] *Ibid.*, p. 187.
[9] *Ibid.*
[10] *Ibid.*, p. 20.

in any absolute (i.e., nonrelative) sense. What is true, as I argued earlier, is that unless causal responsibility for some events is attributed to agents, not to prior causes, then nothing is being described as an action.

Prichard does appear to assume, at least at this stage in his argument, that actions are divided into two mutually exclusive kinds, those in which we originate something directly and those in which we originate something indirectly. The account of action as "bringing about" therefore must apply to actions in the strict sense if it applies at all. But "though on certain occasions we do bring about something, yet there is no kind of activity consisting in bringing something about."[11] Prichard's arguments for this conclusion provide both his ground for rejecting the view of action from which he started and the basis of his own account of action. He offers a different though related argument in "Duty and Ignorance of Fact" from that in "Acting, Willing, Desiring." I will begin with the argument in the former.

Take an action in the strict sense, such as moving my hand. " '*How* did I move it?' " cannot mean " 'By directly causing what, did I cause what I did?' "—"because *ex hypothesi* I am not thinking of the action as one in which I caused some particular thing by causing something else. The legitimate question is: 'What was the activity by performing which I caused my hand to move?' and an answer would be 'Willing the existence of the movement.' And . . . so . . . what I called moving my hand really consisted in setting myself to move it, and . . . I referred to this activity as moving my hand because I thought that this activity had a change of place of my hand as an effect." The activity of setting myself to do something "is a special *kind* of activity, and indeed a special kind of *mental* activity," . . . "of the special nature of which we are aware in performing it." Moreover, if we were to set ourselves to move our arms we

11 *Ibid.*, p. 32.

could not be sure that we would move them, since "we never know that we have not become paralysed."[12] But we would expect to do so, and probably would do so.

The argument in the preceding paragraph is intended to show that contrary to what "we ordinarily think . . . there is no kind of activity consisting in bringing something about,"[13] i.e., bringing something about directly. But it is a premise of the argument that moving my hand is an action in the strict sense, i.e., that the movement of my hand is a change that I bring about directly. The argument could succeed therefore only by showing that the idea of bringing something about is self-contradictory; and it certainly does not do that. It is because it is a premise of the argument that moving my hand is an action in the strict sense that the question "How did I move my hand?" (i.e., "By directly causing what, did I cause what I did?") cannot be asked. It *would* be appropriate to ask "Why did my hand move?", the answer being "My hand moved because I moved it." This answer does not point to a prior event that caused my hand to move; it simply confirms the fact that moving my hand was an action that I performed. And it would also be appropriate to ask "Who moved my hand?", the answer being "I did."

However, despite his assumption that moving my hand is an action in the strict sense, Prichard still feels the need to relate the movement of my hand to something else that brought it about; and he therefore insists on asking "How did I move my hand?" But, since he has not explicitly withdrawn the assumption that moving my hand is an action in the strict sense, he cannot ask it in its original form. "The legitimate question," he says, is "By performing what did I cause my hand to move?"; and his answer is by performing the special kind of mental activity that he calls "setting myself to move my hand." And he concludes that to per-

12 *Ibid.*, pp. 31–34, *passim.*
13 *Ibid.*, pp. 19 and 32.

form this activity is to do an action. But it is not clear what he was looking for in asking this new question; and therefore it is not clear how to interpret his answer. It would be natural to take setting myself to do something as the cause of an action in the strict sense. But Prichard says it is itself an action. When, therefore, I move my hand, though I bring about a change in the position of my hand, I do so indirectly by performing an action of another sort, i.e., setting myself to move my hand. Moving my hand, therefore, is not after all an action in the strict sense, so that the activity I perform in setting myself to move my hand cannot be the cause of an action in the strict sense.

The next interpretation that suggests itself is that setting myself to move my hand is itself an action in the strict sense; if so, in performing it I bring something about directly. But, Prichard says, "though on certain occasions we do bring about something, yet there is no kind of activity consisting in bringing something about."[14] If this is not self-contradictory it must mean that though we sometimes bring things about indirectly (as when I move my hand), we never bring things about directly. There is no such thing as bringing about directly and, therefore, no such thing as an action in the strict sense, as previously defined. Setting one-self to do something cannot therefore be an action in the strict sense.

Prichard's conclusion seems to be that setting myself to do something is an action by performing which I probably bring about something (i.e., a bodily movement) indirectly but bring about nothing directly. But any attraction that this view has depends on showing that "there is no kind of activity consisting in bringing something about"; and this has not been done. I will look at his second argument for this conclusion in the later article "Acting, Willing, Desiring."

"Unquestionably," he says there, "the thing meant by 'an

14 *Ibid.*, p. 32.

action' is an activity. This is so whether we speak of a man's action in moving his hand, or of a body's action such as that of the heart in pumping the blood, or that of one electron in repelling another." He then goes on to compare "a man's action" and "a body's action"; to distinguish, that is, between those events that are human actions and those events that are natural events. He uses as an example of the former "a man's action in moving his hand"; and of the latter the action of "one electron in repelling another" or the sun's action "in attracting the earth." We think both "that some man in moving his hand" and "the sun in attracting the earth, causes a certain movement." But "we do not think that the man's or the sun's activity *is* or *consists in* causing the movement." Just as it was argued in the earlier article that there was no such activity as "bringing about," here again Prichard denies that there is "such an activity as originating or causing a change in something else"; though "the causing a change may require an activity, it is not itself an activity." He then goes on to distinguish between actions and other events in terms of the kind of activity a change requires. We do not know what kind of activity is required when one body causes another to move; "when we speak of a force of attraction or of repulsion we are only expressing our knowledge that there is some activity at work, while being ignorant of what the kind of activity is. In the case, however, of a man, i.e., really, of a man's mind, the matter is different. For example, when we think of ourselves as having moved our hand, we are thinking of ourselves as having performed an activity of a certain kind, and, it almost goes without saying, a *mental* activity of a certain kind, an activity of whose nature we were dimly aware in doing the action, and of which we can become more clearly aware by reflecting on it." Prichard calls this activity willing.[15]

It is not clear in this argument whether Prichard is think-

---

[15] *Ibid.*, pp. 188–89, *passim.*

ing of a cause as an event or a thing. I suggested earlier that it is events that cause other natural events, as in the example of the heavy rainfall that caused a landslide. Of course, the rain's activity did not *"consist in* causing the movement" of the rocks; there is, as Prichard says, no activity that consists *simply* in "causing a change in something else."[16] But it does not follow that we do not know the kind of activity that was involved; it was the activity within the event (i.e., the rainfall) to which we pointed as the cause of the landslide, i.e., the physical movement of the water as the rain fell from the sky onto the hillside. We may not know what activity is involved when one electron repels another or the sun attracts the earth; but if not, this is because we happen to be ignorant of the processes involved in these particular cases. Prichard's view, however, is that whenever one body causes another to move, there is always, besides the physical movement of the bodies, another activity involved of which we are necessarily ignorant; so that when the rain caused the landslide, both the rainfall and some other activity, the causing of the landslide, were involved. This view seems more plausible if a cause is thought of as a thing rather than an event. But the rainfall and the cause of the landslide are both events and, moreover, the same event, though we refer to the rainfall as the cause of the landslide only when explaining why the landslide occurred. There are no things that have the status of causes, whether events or things, independent of any explanatory context. Prichard appears to think that there are, but that in the case of natural events we have no knowledge of them. "In the case, however, of a man, i.e., really, of a man's mind, the matter is different." In that case the activity involved when we cause something is mental, and therefore we are "dimly aware of it . . . and . . . can become more clearly aware of it by reflecting on it."[17] But

---

[16] *Ibid.*, p. 188.
[17] *Ibid.*

he is led to posit the existence of this activity, which he calls willing, not because he has reflected on his own actions and invariably found it, but by his arguments. The grounds for thinking that there are such things as acts of will, therefore, are a priori not empirical.

What then is the special kind of mental activity that was first called "setting myself to move my hand" and is now called "willing a movement of my hand"? I concluded earlier that it is an action by performing which I probably cause some change in the position of my hand indirectly but bring about no change directly. Prichard seems to be operating with the idea of an event that may cause change but that does not itself involve change. But this hardly seems to make sense. If I move my hand to kill a fly I change the position of my hand even if I fail to kill the fly. But if I will a movement of my hand and, being paralyzed, fail to move my hand, then apparently, nothing happens. But if nothing happens there is no event—not even a mental event —of which I can be aware, dimly or otherwise; and the world of the mind cannot be as shadowy as that. Prichard's special mental activities therefore appear to have the peculiar status of causes that are not also events. And they are also privileged in retaining their status as causes even when they do not cause anything; their causal status is independent of any context of explanation.

3. Further Criticism of Prichard's Account

I have tried to explain Prichard's account of action as a special mental activity of setting ourselves to bring about or willing some change. On this view what we ordinarily call an action is a bodily movement caused by a mental act of will. Both the view itself and the Cartesian account of mind that it presupposes have been the subject of criticism in recent years.

In *The Concept of Mind* Professor Ryle points out that "the concept of volition . . . is an artificial concept"[18] and, moreover, like "phlogiston," one that has no legitimate use. Volitions, thought of as the hidden causes of observable behavior, are part of a more general view of the mind that he calls "Descartes' myth . . . the official doctrine," or "the para-mechanical theory of mind."[19] And that view, he says, is radically mistaken, since it places mental concepts in the wrong logical categories. "According to the doctrine, minds belong to the same category as bodies." "Minds are things, but different sorts of things from bodies; mental processes are causes and effects, but different sorts of causes and effects from bodily movements." Of course, the Cartesian account explicitly contrasts minds with bodies; but, Ryle says, minds can be characterized only negatively by describing the ways in which their workings are not like those of bodies— "they are not in space, they are not motions, they are not modifications of matter, they are not accessible to public observation. Minds are not bits of clockwork, they are just bits of not-clockwork."[20] The picture drawn is like that of a severely damaged plane coming in to land—the wings drop off, then the engines, and the tail; just before it lands the body falls off. But it makes no difference; it lands just the same, though not surprisingly, it is no longer publicly observable. Despite its disabilities, the mind is nevertheless supposed to function like a physical body in providing the internal causes of external behavior. The view of a person that results therefore is that of "a ghost mysteriously ensconced in a machine"; and the ghost is itself "just a spectral machine." Ryle therefore calls the Cartesian theory "a para-mechanical hypothesis."[21] And the question is whether the

18 Ryle, *The Concept of Mind,* p. 62.
19 *Ibid.,* pp. 11 and 64.
20 *Ibid.,* pp. 19–20, *passim.*
21 *Ibid.,* pp. 18, 19, and 20.

emaciated wreck of a body that is a mind can play the causal role cast for it.

Ryle's account is not specifically directed at Prichard, but clearly Prichard's basic position is similar to that attacked. If Ryle's attack on the Cartesian account of mind had been wholly successful it would have been possible to argue that volitions cannot be mental events since there are no such things as mental events (in the strong, Cartesian sense of "mental"). But it is not easy to deny the occurrence of at least some mental events, such as pains, mental images, and after-images, or to deny that the person who experiences them is specially placed to report on them. Nor, indeed, does Ryle consistently do so; for example, he admits the occurrence of bodily sensations, when, say, a man's finger is pricked.[22] Nevertheless, Ryle has clearly undermined the Cartesian position.

Moreover, Ryle also puts forward specific arguments to show that there are no mental events that are volitions. For, according to Prichard, every piece of behavior is preceded by a volition "of the special nature of which we are aware in performing it."[23] One would expect, therefore, reports of their occurrence to be readily available. But Ryle says they are not; "ordinary men never report the occurrence of these acts, for all that, according to the theory, they should be encountered vastly more frequently than headaches, or feelings of boredom."[24]

Ryle also argues that if a volition is itself an action "then it must issue from a prior volition and that from another ad infinitum." Similarly, Professor A. I. Melden argues that since there is a difference between the occurrence of an act of will and my performance of it, the latter itself requires a prior act of willing, and so on.[25] But Prichard at least

22 *Ibid.*, p. 84.
23 Prichard, *Moral Obligation*, p. 34.
24 Ryle, *The Concept of Mind*, p. 65.
25 *Ibid.*, p. 67; Melden, *Free Action*, p. 45.

does not say that every action must be preceded by a prior act of will. His view is that, philosophically speaking, volitions, and only volitions, *are* actions. What we ordinarily call an action is an action in this narrow philosophical sense together with a bodily movement caused by it. A bodily movement therefore is not itself an action but counts as part of an action in this everyday sense only if it is caused by an act of will. The only regress in which Prichard is involved is that from an event to its cause, from the cause to its cause, and so on; and this is perfectly acceptable. Prichard does not need to distinguish between a volition's occurring and my performance of it, since he has already given his account of action in pointing to a volition rather than a bodily movement. Melden sees this as only a change in the locus of action, leaving the main problem unsolved. But on the Cartesian view a person is identified primarily with his mind, not with his body. Therefore though a distinction must be made between the occurrence of a bodily movement and my moving my body, there is not the same need to make a similar distinction between the occurrence of a mental event and my performing it.

A further difficulty, to which Prichard himself draws attention, is that the special mental activity in performing which we perform an action is not "describable by itself" but "solely by reference to something else,"[26] i.e., by reference to what, on some occasions, is caused by it. For example, the act of will whereby I move my arm can be described only as an act of willing a movement of my arm. There is therefore an unavoidable conceptual or logical connection between the mental cause and its effect. But, Melden argues, a cause, "whether mental or physiological, . . . must be logically distinct from its alleged effect."[27] It is not clear, however, why this must be so. Things may be contingently related even though one is described in terms

---

[26] Prichard, *Moral Obligation*, p. 35.
[27] Melden, *Free Action*, p. 53.

of the other, for example fire engines and fires, mayflies and May, or, to use an example of Mill's, Dartmouth and the mouth of the Dart. In these examples an independent description could be produced; it is doubtful whether this could be done for volitions. But if not this is either because there are no such things as volitions or because of the general difficulty of producing a public description of a private mental event. Melden's argument therefore is not conclusive.

A final problem, which Descartes himself admitted, is how in view of their distinct natures the body and the mind can interact; how, that is, a mental event that is temporal but nonspatial can cause a physical event that is both spatial and temporal. Volitions cannot therefore be both mental events and causes of bodily movement; but in Prichard's account they are both. This, I think, is the objection to which Ryle attaches most importance. "Minds, as the whole legend describes them, are what must exist if there is to be a causal explanation of the intelligent behaviour of human bodies; and minds, as the legend describes them, live on a floor of existence defined as being outside the causal system."[28] Moreover, if acts of will are thought of as autonomous, i.e., as uncaused causes, the difficulty is compounded. For they are then events that in being mental themselves avoid being caused while remaining potent as causes of physical events. In Prichard's account willing occurs as a result of desiring to will; Prichard himself therefore does not have to meet this final difficulty.

Despite the authority of both Descartes and Ryle, I cannot see any a priori reason why mental events should not cause physical events. Provided it is admitted that both occur, it must be admitted also that they are related in some way. And it seems obvious that physical events can cause mental events, for example, when someone is pricked by a pin, or when the central nervous system is subjected to

[28] Ryle, *The Concept of Mind*, p. 66.

direct physical, chemical, or electrical stimulation, as in the work of Penfield. For me the fundamental objection to Prichard's account is that if he were right I should be able to recognize in my own experience the occurrence of acts of will. But I can't; indeed, despite my best efforts to find out what a volition is, I don't even know what to look for.

CHAPTER III

Actions and Bodily Movements

1. Actions as a Subclass of Bodily Movements

I want to return now to the view of what a person is, which I mentioned at the beginning of the previous chapter, in which a person is identified with his body. If this alternative is adopted, actions are likely to be thought of as movements of human bodies, i.e., bodily movements. Some bodily movements, however, are the direct result of external causes; the example given in Chapter I was the movement of Brutus' arm caused by a rock falling from a cliff. And presumably such movements would not count as actions.

Our willingness to say that Brutus' arm moved because Brutus moved it—and therefore to accept the movement of his arm as an action—seemed to depend on the fact that, as far as we know, nothing external to Brutus caused his arm to move. But all cases of physical interaction are not as simple as the model of the interaction of balls on a billiard table suggests. Perhaps if we look more carefully we can relate all movements of Brutus' arm to prior events, events that differ only in complexity from the falling rock that served as an obvious external cause of the movement of Brutus' arm. There would then be no obvious grounds for picking out a special subclass of the movements of Brutus' body and referring to them as actions.

Even in the case of the rock, there may have been no obvious reason why it should have fallen from the cliff at that precise moment. Nevertheless, we have no inclination to say that it moved itself; rather, we assume that its movement was the product of an accumulation of small changes —the erosion of the soil supporting it, pressure of plant roots, and so on. Moreover, some things are internally complex. They are made up of parts that are related to one another in complex physical and chemical ways. The movements of the hands of a watch, for example, are caused by the gradual uncoiling of a spring concealed behind the watch face. The source of movement of the hands lies, therefore, at least partly within the watch. Artifacts that are capable of moving about can also be constructed; for example, clockwork railway engines.

Considerations of this sort led Hobbes to conclude that a machine is an artificial animal. "For seeing life is but a motion of limbs, the beginning whereof is in some principal part within; why may we not say, that all *automata* (engines that move themselves by springs and wheels as doth a watch) have an artificial life? For what is the *heart*, but a *spring*; and the *nerves*, but so many *strings*; and the *joints*, but so many *wheels*, giving motion to the whole body, such as was intended by the artificer?"[1] If this view is correct, then the movement of Brutus' arm when Brutus moved his arm, and the movement of Brutus' arm when it was hit by a rock, can both be related to prior events that were causally responsible, in precisely the same sense, for their occurrence.

Nor is Hobbes' view of historical interest only. Professor

[1] Hobbes, *Leviathan*, Introduction.

R. S. Peters has drawn attention to the similarity between the views of Hobbes and those of C. L. Hull, the American psychologist; and to the latter's ambition "of starting from 'colorless movements and mere receptor impulses as such' and eventually explaining everything"—that is, all aspects of human behavior including actions—"in terms of such concepts."[2] This sort of view is shared by many modern psychologists and physiologists; indeed, there are indisputable facts about the human body that make it very attractive. The human body consists of a skeletal framework, operated by muscles and powered by oxygen from the lungs and food from the stomach. Parts of it, such as the eye, are especially sensitive or irritable, and enter into physical interaction with their environments on a "miniature" scale. The physical energy involved when light is reflected from the surface of a physical object is small; but the eye is sensitive to small amounts of energy. And the brain, another part of the body, is capable of analyzing and storing the patterns of energy that fall on the eye and other sensory receptors. Biological organisms are not only capable of initiating and providing the energy for their own movements, but are also able to orient their movements in relation to relevant features of their previous experience and present environment. Their movements therefore are adapted, in general, to the preservation of their separate identities in the face of external forces that would otherwise destroy them.

Bodily movements may therefore occur as the end result of a complex pattern of events both within and external to the body. And if an action is a bodily movement caused in this way, then the difference between an action and a bodily movement that is not an action is merely one of complexity.

[2] Peters, *The Concept of Motivation*, p. 2.

2. *Behaviorism in Psychology*

There is a danger at this point of confusing purely philosophic views with methodological prescriptions for psychological inquiry. For example, to think of the mind as a stream of sensations or ideas is to have a view about what a mind is; and such a view is philosophical. It is also likely to lead to a view of the proper method of conducting empirical investigations in psychology; and historically this is in fact what happened. David Hartley and James Mill, and their successors in the nineteenth century, thought of psychology as the study of the phenomena of the human mind, and tried to formulate the laws that govern them. Their data consisted of observations of their own conscious experiences and, later, of the verbal reports of others. The appropriate method for psychology was therefore introspection.

Early in this century, however, J. B. Watson rejected introspection as unscientific, since one person's report of the content of his mind cannot be checked by another. Instead, psychology should concern itself only with what is publicly observable, that is, the physical environment of an organism (animal or man) and changes in it and the physical body of the organism and its movements. Psychology was the science not of mind but of behavior, correlating changes in the environment—the stimulus situation—with observable responses of the organism. Accordingly, the psychologist should stop using terms like "consciousness," "mental states," and "imagery" and instead confine himself to the vocabulary of stimulus and response, movement, habit formation, and so on. Only in this way could psychology achieve success in the prediction and control of behavior.

A simple example may make the point clearer. Cows can be kept in a field by an electric fence. At first they may brush against it; but when they do so they receive an electric shock and soon learn to keep away. It may then even be possible to switch the electric current off. This is all the farmer needs to know in order to control the behavior of his cows. A conscious state—an experience of pain—may or may not intervene between the subsequent behavior of the cows and the electrical stimulus that they received when their bodies touched the fence. But if so, a reference to such a state plays no part in explaining their behavior. Mental concepts may be rejected therefore because they have no part to play in psychological explanation. But a behaviorist position on methodology can be adopted without also adopting the sort of philosophic position that I attributed to Hobbes. It is important to distinguish between methodological behaviorism in psychology and philosophic views with which it may be associated. It is the latter only that I wish to consider here.

3. *Physicalism*

Views similar to those of Hobbes have been expressed recently by Professor J. J. C. Smart in *Philosophy and Scientific Realism*. In his view the job of the philosopher is to try "to acquire a synoptic view of the world," deciding "between various synoptic hypotheses on grounds of plausibility."[3] Simplicity plays a part in deciding what is plausible, especially Ockham's razor, the precept that entities are not to be multiplied beyond necessity. But Smart himself attaches most importance to what is plausible in the light of modern scientific knowledge. "It looks today," he says,

[3] Smart, *Philosophy and Scientific Realism*, pp. 3 and 8.

"as though the ultimate laws of nature are those of physics"; and he argues "that the physicist's language gives us a truer picture of the world than does the language of common sense."[4] Biology and psychology "are an application of physics and chemistry to natural history"; and "living organisms, including human beings, are simply complicated physico-chemical mechanisms."[5] The "disguised anthropocentricity" that "still prevails in many fields of philosophy" is rejected in favor of the view that man "is nothing more than a complicated physical mechanism."[6]

Smart thinks that most psychological concepts are "capable of behaviouristic or quasi-behaviouristic analysis"[7] along the lines suggested by Ryle in *The Concept of Mind.* But Ryle recognized the occurrence of some conscious experiences, though minimizing their importance, and, therefore, failed to eliminate the two-worlds myth. Smart too admits that "many of our ordinary psychological concepts seem to refer to inner processes"; when, for example, "I report that I am having an orange-yellow roundish after-image . . . or that I have a pain."[8] Conscious experiences are thus a major obstacle for any account of man simply as a complex physical mechanism and, therefore, for a physicalist world-view. Smart therefore argues that "our conscious experiences are to be identified with brain processes"[9] and that the brain itself is no more than a physical machine.

If the exceptions were confined to the examples Smart gives, it would not be necessary to consider his argument here. But it may be argued that when I perform an action I am aware of, or conscious of, what I am doing; and that any account of action that ignores this is incomplete. When Brutus stabbed Caesar he knew what he was doing and

[4] *Ibid.*, pp. 68 and 47.
[5] *Ibid.*, pp. 64 and 20.
[6] *Ibid.*, p. 15.
[7] *Ibid.*, p. 89.
[8] *Ibid.*, pp. 88 and 89.
[9] *Ibid.*, p. 11.

intended to do it. Professor D. W. Hamlyn argues in this
way in "Causality and Human Behaviour." "It is," he says,
"a general necessary condition of applying to anything the
conceptual scheme which centres round the concept of action that the thing in question should be conscious."[10] The
most important concept in that scheme is that of an intention; it is the intention with which a person acts that provides the criterion of identity of an action. It is because
Brutus intended to kill Caesar when he stabbed him that
his action is identified as killing Caesar, and not as merely
moving his arm. He had a reason for stabbing Caesar; he
wanted Caesar dead. The notion of a reason for acting is
closely related to that of an intention. And, since intentions
presuppose awareness or consciousness, the agent knows,
without observation, what his intentions are. Thus an agent
is the best authority on what his intentions, and therefore
his actions, are. Hamlyn makes no causal claim for consciousness—"as far as bodily movement is concerned, physiological theory is complete in principle." But he insists that
"consciousness is conceptually necessary for action."[11]
Whatever the attractions of this view, it is clear that it faces
the sort of epistemological difficulty stressed by Ryle in discussing the doctrine of volitions. How can I ever know that
the condition on which the application of action concepts
depends—that the thing to which they are applied is conscious—is satisfied except in my own case? If consciousness
is a brain process it would be possible, at least in principle,
to observe someone else's brain processes and therefore to
know that someone else was conscious; but in practice we
apply action concepts to others without first slicing off the
tops of their heads and inspecting the contents.

10 Hamlyn, "Causality and Human Behavior," p. 138.
11 *Ibid.*, pp. 128 and 141.

4. *The Identity Theory*

Smart acknowledges a debt to an article "Is Consciousness a Brain Process?" written by a psychologist, U. T. Place. In that article Place puts forward "the thesis that consciousness is a process in the brain . . . as a reasonable scientific hypothesis, not to be dismissed on logical grounds alone."[12] Therefore "consciousness is a brain process" is to be understood as a contingent proposition, the truth of which is to be established experimentally. In studying the perception of color Place would presumably be content to confine himself to what was publicly observable, correlating changes in the stimulus situation—the presentation of different colors—with the subject's observable responses. In this way it could be established whether an experimental subject—man, rat, or bee—was seeing, e.g., a yellow patch, without relying on introspective data. The conscious experience involved in seeing a yellow patch, if any, can be ignored as playing no part in the explanation of the behavior of the subject, just as the cow's behavior in avoiding the electric fence can be explained without referring to the pain, if any, that the cow experiences when its body touches the fence. The difficulty arises when a subject reports seeing an after-image; his behavior can no longer be explained as a response to a yellow patch, for there is no yellow patch present. How then is it to be explained? When we report seeing a green after-image, Place says, "we are saying that we are having the sort of experience which we normally have when, and which we have learnt to describe

[12] Place, "Is Consciousness a Brain Process?" *British Journal of Psychology,* XLV, 1954, p. 44.

as, looking at a green patch of light."[13] In his account, Smart avoids using the word "experience," which might be thought question-begging. According to him, when we report a yellowish-orange after-image what we report is in effect *" 'What is going on in me is like what is going on in me when* my eyes are open, the lighting is normal, etc., etc., and there really is a yellowish-orange patch on the wall.' "[14] The italicized words are, he says, topic-neutral. Thus the question of what is going on in me when I report seeing a yellow after-image is left open. And the identity hypothesis is that as a matter of fact what is going on in me is a brain process. The "is" here is the "is" of identity, as in "the morning star is (identical with) the evening star."

The hypothesis can be tested experimentally by correlating a subject's overt responses to actual yellow patches with neural processes in his brain—the responses, the yellow patches, and the neural processes all being publicly observable. Once this is done the brain processes that occur when a subject reports seeing a yellow after-image can be observed. It can then be decided whether they are in fact the same as those that occur when an actual yellow patch is seen. If they are then, as Place points out, "all the physiologist or physiological psychologist has to do in order to explain the subject's introspective observations, is to show that the brain process which is causing the subject to describe his experiences in this way, is the sort of process which normally occurs when he is observing an actual"[15] yellow patch. In this way the behaviorist psychologist can provide an explanation of after-images without violating his methodological principles, i.e., without relying on introspective data. Similarly, it could be argued that when I reported feeling as though I were stabbing Caesar (perhaps in some

[13] *Ibid.,* p. 49.
[14] Smart, *Philosophy and Scientific Realism,* p. 94.
[15] Place, "Is Consciousness a Brain Process?" p. 50.

sort of delirium) the same sort of brain processes occurred that would occur if I were actually stabbing Caesar.

The fact that explanations of this sort are possible does not itself refute philosophical dualism. For that it would be necessary to claim that nothing is left out of these explanations. Smart, for example, says that "sensations, states of consciousness, do seem to be the one sort of thing left outside the physicalist picture, and for various reasons I just cannot believe that this can be so."[16] That this is also Place's position is clear from the explanation he gives of the logical status of "consciousness is a brain process." Though it is not a definition, he says, it is like a definition in that the words "and nothing else" can be added. For example, the words "and nothing else" could be added to "the morning star is the evening star" or "her hat is a bundle of straw tied together with string."[17] Here the words "and nothing else" must mean "and there are no other physical components such as feathers or cloth." Similarly, it might be said that a rainbow is refracted light and nothing else, i.e., is not made of painted candy floss that you can eat if you get close enough. "Consciousness is a brain process" therefore is to be understood in the same way, that is, consciousness is a brain process and nothing else, i.e., nothing mental.

If this thesis is to be established it needs to be shown not only that when we report seeing a yellow after-image what we are reporting is that what is going on is like what goes on when we see an actual yellow patch; but also that when we report seeing an actual yellow patch what we report is not "something irreducibly psychical."[18] In his article Place not only departs from methodological behaviorism at this point (in itself a sensible enough thing to

[16] Smart, "Sensations and Brain Process," *The Philosophy of Mind*, p. 142.

[17] Place, "Is Consciousness a Brain Process?" p. 45.

[18] Smart, "Sensations and Brain Process," p. 142.

do), but he also begs the philosophical question by talking about "introspective observations reported by the subject."[19] Smart, however, analyzes color concepts in terms of "the discriminatory responses of normal percipients," so that a congenitally blind man could fully understand the use of color words, though unable to make color discriminations himself.[20] In short, Smart argues that what goes on when a normal percipient sees a yellow patch under normal conditions is that a characteristic brain process occurs and nothing else, i.e., no "irreducibly psychical" event occurs also. And presumably the subject is able to report the occurrence of such a brain process by means of a self-scanning mechanism within the brain, and can therefore report the occurrence of such a process when it occurs in the absence of its usual cause, the presentation of a yellow patch.

An objection anticipated by Smart is that people can report seeing yellow patches or yellow after-images even though they know nothing of brain processes. This is possible, Smart says, because the reports are really to the effect that "there is something going on which is like what is going on" when a color discrimination is made, and such reports are "topic-neutral." And Smart claims that I can say that two things, including two neurological processes, are alike without being able to mention the properties in virtue of which they are alike; just as "a person may say 'someone is in the room,' thus reporting truly that the doctor is in the room, even though he had never heard of doctors."[21] But this analogy does not work; "someone" means some person, and persons are publicly observable and can be described in lots of ways. Though I may not know that the person in the room is the doctor, I must know something about him, e.g., that he is wearing a shabby suit, has gray hair, and so

[19] Place, "Is Consciousness a Brain Process?" p. 48.

[20] Smart, *Philosophy and Scientific Realism,* p. 80. Details of the example on p. 79, foot, to p. 81.

[21] ———"Sensations and Brain Processes," p. 150.

on. Therefore if we can say that two neurological processes
are alike and admit also that we are not saying that they are
alike in possessing common neurological (i.e., physical)
properties, it remains possible that the comparison is made
on the basis of mental properties.

The difference between Smart and Hamlyn reflects an
ambiguity in the notion of consciousness, or awareness, itself. Suppose I am sitting in the library reading. At first I
concentrate on what I am doing, though occasionally my
attention wanders and I look about me. Later I get sleepy
and doze off, dreaming briefly of a kind, gentle girl who
caresses my brow. In the evening a friend comments on the
pretty girl I kept looking at in the library. "What girl?" I
ask; how could he have known about the kind, gentle girl
in my dream? My friend explains, somewhat skeptically,
that he is talking about the fair-haired girl in the miniskirt
sitting by the window. I say that I was aware of no such
girl; he replies, "Well, you looked in her direction often
enough." In this example there are two distinct, though related, notions at work. While awake I am aware of what is
going on around me and pay attention to the features of
the environment relevant to my needs and interests. In this
sense of "aware" I cannot be aware of what is not there;
hence my reply, "What girl?" But of course there was a girl,
and I showed that I was aware of her by looking in her
direction. When asleep, however, I pay no attention to my
surroundings, but I am not therefore unconscious. Indeed, I
was pleasantly conscious of the kind, gentle girl who ca-
ressed my brow, even though, outside my dream, there is
no such girl. She was of the stuff that dreams are made of;
to use Brentano's expression, she possessed only intentional
inexistence.[22] Smart is thinking of consciousness primarily
in the former sense of awareness; Hamlyn is thinking of it
primarily in the latter, or strong, sense. This is shown in

[22] Brentano, "The Distinction Between Mental and Physical Phenomena" in *Realism and the Background of Phenomenology*, p. 50.

Hamlyn's insistence that there is something else, in addition to overt or, indeed, covert behavior to be taken into account; and in Smart's assumption that consciousness presents a problem only in the case of after-images that appear to have the same sort of intentional inexistence as the kind, gentle girl in my dream.

Smart's claim is that when I report seeing an after-image or a girl in a dream what I am aware of is a brain process; the evidence that I am aware of it is my verbal behavior. In my example, however, I was aware of the fair-haired girl in the miniskirt since, according to my friend, I kept looking at her; but I was not in a position to give a verbal report of this fact, since I was not aware that I was aware of her. The same sort of brain process occurred as when I was aware of the girl in my dream; but I was unaware of this. My looking at the fair-haired girl, therefore, was a response to a girl; my saying that I dreamed of a kind, gentle girl was a response to a brain process, since in Smart's sense I cannot be aware of what is not there. Why then in the case of the fair-haired girl am I not aware of both a brain process and a girl? Presumably I could have been; but awareness of a brain process requires the operation of a self-scanning mechanism in the brain, and this mechanism did not in fact scan the brain process caused by the girl in the library. Otherwise I would not have denied being aware of her.

It is a consequence of Hamlyn's position, therefore, that people are in a privileged position so far as the content of their own minds is concerned; but it is also a consequence of Smart's position that people are in a privileged position so far as the processes going on in their own brains is concerned. In the former case they are necessarily privileged; in the latter case only contingently so, since their brain processes could be observed by a neurophysiologist. This means that physicalism is not as vulnerable as it at first seems to be to arguments based on the self-knowledge that is, in Miss Anscombe's phrase, knowledge without observation.[23] Privileged self-knowledge is something that physicalism is very well able to account for.

Smart's arguments are designed to show "that there are no cogent philosophical arguments which force us into accepting dualism." If, as he thinks, there aren't, then the issue is to be decided on grounds of plausibility, i.e., on whether conscious experience, understood as something irreducibly mental, can be fitted "in any plausible way, into the body of our scientific knowledge."[24] But only if physicalism is accepted is science the sole arbiter of what is plausible; and if science is not the sole arbiter, then the identity theory as a philosophic account of consciousness is wholly implausible. What it does do is show that it is possible to offer a scientific explanation of reports of after-images, dreams, and so on that makes no *mention* of consciousness.

5. Ryle's Account of Intelligent Performance

Most mental concepts, in Smart's view, can be analyzed behavioristically, without any reference to consciousness, along the lines suggested by Ryle in *The Concept of Mind*; and his own arguments in Chapter 6 of his book are designed to show that there is no reason why a machine should not have "the human sort of intelligence," i.e., "the sort of purposefulness, appropriateness, and adaptiveness that is characteristic of human beings." In other words, he tries to show that mental concepts, as analyzed by Ryle, could apply to machines as well as to men. His arguments are designed to show that "it might one day be possible, though somewhat pointless, to build an artifact which behaved in

[23] Anscombe, G. E. M., *Intention*, p. 13.
[24] Smart, "Sensations and Brain Process," pp. 156 and 68.

every way just like a man."[25] And if the identity hypothesis is accepted, such a being would also be conscious.

There is, he says, no a priori reason why the "ingenuity problem"[26] of building a machine capable of solving problems for which there is no algorithm or decision procedure should not be solved. But I do not propose to consider Smart's arguments in detail. For what would it prove if men could create robots in their own image? The result would be little different from supposing that the story of the creation of man by God were true. Human beings may in the future come to occupy the position of Homeric gods, no doubt disgusting their own creations with their gross carnality, lusts, and destructiveness. Philosophically minded robots would still need to ask the sort of questions now being asked about men. What, for example, is the difference between a robot's raising his arm and his arm being raised when he inadvertently walked under an electromagnet? Given an answer to the question "What is it to perform an action?" it remains a contingent matter which beings may properly be said to perform actions.

The point of comparisons between men and machines, therefore, depends on a prior philosophical analysis of mental concepts. Questions about whether machines capable of doing certain things are possible can be answered only if what they are required to do is clear; the answer then depends only on the technical possibilities. What remains important is the positive account of mental concepts on which Smart relies, i.e., that given by Ryle. Ryle does not *deny* that mental phenomena occur; his intention is to give an analysis of the logic of the sentences we use to talk about them. Descartes, he says, misunderstood the logic of his problem. Instead of asking by what criteria intelligent behavior is actually distinguished from nonintelligent behavior, he asked, "Given that the principle of mechanical cau-

[25] Smart, *Philosophy and Scientific Realism*, pp. 107 and 109.
[26] *Ibid.*, p. 115.

sation does not tell us the difference, what other causal principle will tell it to us?" For we can all already "recognise the difference between, say, rational and non-rational utterances or between purposive and automatic behaviour"; between, that is, "a man and a Robot."[27] Mental predicates do not refer to "occult causes" of what people say and do but are used to describe "the ways in which people conduct parts of their predominantly public behaviour." We go beyond what we see, but only "in the sense of considering, in the first instance, the powers and propensities of which their actions are exercises."[28]

In the second chapter of *The Concept of Mind* Ryle applies this general theme to "that family of . . . mental-conduct concepts . . . ordinarily surnamed 'intelligence'" which includes "'clever,' 'sensible,' 'careful,'" and many others; it also includes those attributing stupidity or deficiency in intelligence such as "dull," "silly," "careless," and so on. When somebody is described as "intelligent," what is imputed to him is "the ability, or inability, to do certain sorts of things"; he knows, that is, "how to perform tasks." And Ryle insists that knowing how to do something cannot be reduced to knowing that something is the case. "Intelligent practice is not a step-child of theory. On the contrary theorising is one practice amongst others and is itself intelligently or stupidly conducted."[29]

The important distinction is not between intelligent and unintelligent (i.e., stupid) performances but between intelligent and nonintelligent performances. Actions may be described as voluntary or involuntary, intentional or unintentional, successful or unsuccessful, moral or immoral, as well as intelligent or stupid; and Ryle discusses some of these distinctions later in the book. But these distinctions apply only to what is already in the right dimension, i.e.,

27 Ryle, *The Concept of Mind*, pp. 20–21, *passim*.
28 *Ibid.*, p. 51.
29 *Ibid.*, pp. 25–28, *passim*.

to actions as opposed to mechanical movements. The important contrast, therefore, is not between knowing how to do something and not really knowing (and, therefore, botching it up), but between intelligent as compared with mechanical performance. This is perhaps obscured by the fact that "know" is what Ryle himself later calls an achievement word—its use incorporates a reference to success. This could be avoided if a corresponding task-word were available. "Believing that you know how"—which leaves open the question of whether you really do know how—is perhaps what is wanted.

Ryle begins his account by denying that "the intelligent execution of an operation must embody two processes, one of doing and another of theorising."[30] Theorizing is the activity of "finding the answers to questions"; its goal is "the knowledge of true propositions or facts." In the view he is attacking, the apprehension of truths is "the defining property of a mind. Other human powers could be classed as mental only if they could be shown to be somehow piloted by the intellectual grasp of true propositions."[31] Reasoning or fishing, for example, are intelligent practices only because the propositions of logic or the precepts of Isaak Walton are known and applied. But, Ryle argues, theorizing itself is an example of knowing how. It is therefore "itself an operation the execution of which can be more or less intelligent, less or more stupid. But if, for any operation to be intelligently executed, a prior theoretical operation had first to be performed and performed intelligently, it would be a logical impossibility for anyone ever to break into the circle." In any case there are many practices, such as humor, or reasoning before Aristotle, "the rules or criteria of which are unformulated";[32] and even where rules exist they are necessarily general and, logically, cannot incorporate complete directions for their own application.

[30] *Ibid.*, p. 32.
[31] *Ibid.*, p. 26.
[32] *Ibid.*, p. 30.

When we describe people as knowing how to perform tasks intelligently, "part of what is meant," according to Ryle, is that "their performances come up to certain standards, or satisfy certain criteria. But this is not enough. The well-regulated clock keeps good time. . . . To be intelligent is not merely to satisfy criteria, but to apply them; to regulate one's actions and not merely to be well-regulated."[33] What, then, is it to apply criteria? A boy is said to know how to play chess if he is "able to make the required moves." It is neither necessary nor sufficient that he should be able "to recite the rules accurately . . . in terms of which 'correct' and 'incorrect' are defined. . . . His knowledge *how* is exercised primarily in the moves that he makes, or concedes, and in the moves that he avoids or vetoes."[34]

A performance is intelligent, then, if it is an exercise of a skill. The movements of a clown in performing his act, for example, are not the "effect of any hidden internal causes"[35] but the exercise of a disposition to make some moves—the correct ones, those that will make the people laugh—and not others—the incorrect ones, those that will not make people laugh. But though we learn how to do things by practice rather than precept, intelligent performance is more than just habit. "It is of the essence of merely habitual practices that one performance is a replica of its predecessors. It is of the essence of intelligent practices that one performance is modified by its predecessors." The scope for continued improvement in skilled performances arises from the fact that skills are not "simple, single-track dispositions, the actualisations of which are nearly uniform" but higher-grade dispositions "the exercises of which are indefinitely heterogeneous," taking "a wide and perhaps unlimited variety of shapes." To say that a man is a cigarette smoker, for example, is not to say that he is now smoking a cigarette; but

33 *Ibid.*, p. 28.
34 *Ibid.*, p. 41.
35 *Ibid.*, p. 33.

it is to say he has a disposition to do just one particular thing —smoke cigarettes. It is therefore to attribute a single-track disposition. But there is no one particular way in which pride is exemplified; it is reflected in "actions, words, thoughts and feelings in a thousand different situations." To say that someone is proud is therefore to attribute a higher-grade disposition.[36]

"Knowing how" includes "knowing how to make and appreciate jokes, to talk grammatically, to play chess, to fish, to argue,"[37] and, importantly, theorizing or finding out truths or facts; anything, in short, that can be said to be done either intelligently or stupidly. Therefore it includes some things that would normally be contrasted with acting, such as thinking or talking, as well as many things that are actions. It is not clear whether it also includes things like putting the kettle on, going for a walk, or drinking beer, which would not usually be regarded as skilled performances; but clearly skill is involved in doing these things, though not obviously so. Ryle's account of knowing how can therefore be taken as including his account of actions.

Before returning to Smart, I will comment briefly on the part played by theorizing in this account. The notion of theorizing was introduced in a technical philosophical sense in which theorizing is attaining knowledge of *any* true propositions. Later, when Ryle argues that intelligent performance need not be preceded by theorizing, "theorizing" is used in a narrow, nontechnical sense in which the theory is contrasted with the practice of a skilled activity as, for example, in "theory and practice of technical drawing, education, or road construction." And it does not follow, because skilled performance in these practices need not be preceded by theorizing in this nontechnical sense, that actions need not be preceded by theorizing in the broad, technical sense in which the notion was introduced. Later (in

36 *Ibid.,* pp. 42–44, *passim.*
37 *Ibid.,* p. 28.

Chapter V, Section 4) I will argue that I cannot be said to
have performed an action unless my action was guided by
my beliefs about the situation in which and on which I
acted.

6. *Dispositions and Physicalism*

Smart claims Ryle as an ally in his attempt to present
man as no more than a "complicated psycho-chemical mechanism"; but it is clear that Ryle himself would not wish to
occupy that role. He says, for example, that "a person's
thinking, feeling and purposive doing cannot be described
solely in the idioms of physics, chemistry and physiology";
and that the fear that everything is "explicable by mechanical laws is a baseless fear."[38] Smart tries to meet this point
by arguing that there is no a priori reason why "an artifact
which behaved in every way just like a man"[39] should not
be constructed; but I have already pointed out that such
arguments do nothing to achieve their purpose. Nevertheless, I think Smart is right in claiming Ryle as an ally, even
though Ryle's own preoccupations are epistemological and
not, like Smart's, metaphysical. It is because "overt intelligent performances are . . . the workings of minds,"[40] not
merely clues to them, that the epistemological problems pre-
sented by Cartesianism are avoided. In describing what
somebody is doing it is true that we are not, according to
Ryle, merely describing the movements of their body. "We
go beyond what we see them do and hear them say," certainly not by "making inferences to occult causes" but by

[38] *Ibid.*, pp. 18 and 76.
[39] Smart, *Philosophy and Scientific Realism*, p. 109.
[40] Ryle, *The Concept of Mind*, p. 58.

"considering, in the first instance, the powers and propensities of which their actions are exercises."[41] Though "doing is often an overt physical affair," it cannot "be written off as a merely physical process,"[42] but only because it is an exercise of a disposition to make just such movements in just such circumstances. But physical things have the dispositional properties that they have only because their physical state is what it is. Rubber, for example, is elastic because it has a certain molecular structure; hot metal burns incautious fingers because it is hot, and so on. The molecular structure of rubber or the state of the molecules in hot metal can be described independently of the dispositional properties that result from them. And there is no reason whatsoever to suppose that human bodies possess the dispositional properties which, on Ryle's analysis, are mental properties independent of their physical states, though the states in question may be neural states of unimaginable complexity. Smart says he is inclined to a "quasi-behaviouristic" analysis of mental concepts "because I would prefer to say, for example, that fear is the state of a person which is the causal condition of the characteristic behaviour pattern, rather than as with Ryle that it is the behaviour pattern."[43] But he need not disagree with Ryle even to this extent; he could say both that to be afraid is to be disposed to behave in certain ways, for example, to run away; and also that, as a matter of fact, this disposition is caused by a bodily state. I conclude therefore that Ryle's account is consistent with physicalism.

It should now be clear also why the philosophic position adopted by Ryle and Smart is attractive to those psychologists who adopt a behaviorist position on methodology. Psychological explanations that make no reference to conscious states can no longer be accused of leaving out of considera-

[41] *Ibid.*, p. 51.
[42] *Ibid.*, p. 32.
[43] Smart, *Philosophy and Scientific Realism*, p. 89.

tion what is most important, since they leave nothing out.
Nor can it be said that, however complete their explanations of bodily movements, they could not provide explanations of actions. For on this view actions are a species of
bodily movements, differing only in complexity from movements caused directly by external causes, as when the rock
fell on Brutus' arm, and reflexes in which the internal me-
diation takes place only within the peripheral nervous
system.

7. The Rule-following Purposive Model

The rule-following purposive model of action as put forward, for example, by Professor R. S. Peters in *The Concept of Motivation,* claims to describe the central features
of actions as they appear to us, rather than saying what they
must be, or really are, if a particular metaphysic or synoptic
world-view such as physicalism is to be consistently maintained. I will first outline the model of action itself and then
consider the claim that it is inconsistent with the physicalist
account of actions as bodily movements.

The most important feature of the account is the stress
on purpose. "The paradigm of a human action," Peters says,
"is when something is done in order to bring about an end."
Actions are therefore to be explained "in terms of a man's
reason for doing something." For example, Jones crossed
the road to buy some tobacco; his reason for crossing the
road was to buy tobacco. Since Jones is "presumed to be
intelligent . . . he will, accordingly, vary his movements in
a great variety of ways" in order to attain his goal. If the
traffic is heavy, for example, he will walk to the intersection
and wait for the go signal; if the traffic is light he may take
the shortest available route. "It is," moreover, "a gross over-

simplification to think of ends merely as terminating points of activity." In this example Jones' end was, in effect, to put himself in a position to perform a further action, that of buying tobacco. Crossing the road is picked out as a means only because the end toward which it is directed is also identified. Similarly, buying some tobacco is picked out as an end of action only because steps were taken to achieve it. Thus "means" and "ends" are correlative terms, each defined in terms of the other. Actions also have further consequences, which may or may not be foreseen by the agent. This is not stressed by Peters, and may not be important in a discussion centered on explanations of actions such as his; but it is important from the point of view of moral philosophy. Finally, Peters contrasts "his reason" for crossing the road (i.e., the reason *he* gives, or would give if he were honest) with "the reason" (i.e., the real reason). For example, Jones may believe that he crossed the road to buy tobacco, which is therefore "his reason;" but "the reason," that is, his real reason, may have been to talk to the girl in the tobacconist's. And, Peters says, "whereas *his* reason—whether real or not—entails that a man is conscious of his objective, the reason why he did it does not."[44]

The second main feature of this account is its stress on social rules. An action is an action of a certain sort only because of its place in a "systematic framework of norms and goals."[45] This point is also stressed by Professor Melden in his article "Action," where he says that "the practical context of common or shared practices involved in following rules, applying criteria, observing principles, acting on policies, and so on . . . is essential to an understanding of the distinction between a bodily movement and an action."[46] Social rules place constraints on both the choice of goals and the means to be adopted in attaining them. Buying tobacco

[44] Peters, *The Concept of Motivation*, pp. 4–13, *passim*.
[45] *Ibid.*, p. 7.
[46] Melden, "Action" in *Philosophical Review* LXV, 1956, p. 536. Also, *Essays in Philosophical Psychology*, ed. D. F. Gustafson, p. 71.

is a socially accepted goal; buying pot or LSD may not be. Similarly, inviting your political rivals to dinner and poisoning them is not the way to political power laid down by the United States Constitution, though it may have been an acceptable political ploy in Renaissance Italy. Some means or ends can be adopted despite the social rules that forbid them, though they are then described in special ways and become actions of a different sort, such as crimes or wicked deeds. Many goals "are defined almost entirely by social convention"; buying tobacco, for example, is defined as an end "because of a vast system of norms" including those governing the ownership and transfer of property. This is even more obviously so with "ends like passing an examination, getting married, becoming a professor, and reading a paper."[47] Indeed, nothing would count as a man's becoming a professor in the absence of the social institution that creates such a role.

Both of these features of actions—their purposive or goal-directed character and their connection with social rules—are taken as giving rise to grounds for saying that "we can never specify an action exhaustively in terms of movements of the body or within the body."[48] First, the principle of identity of an action is provided by the goal toward which it is directed; consequently the means adopted and, therefore, the bodily movements made in performing the action, will vary with the circumstances. This point relies solely on the goal-directed character of actions. Second, we apply to actions concepts that have no application to bodily movements as such; "movements *qua* movements are neither intelligent, efficient, nor correct. They only become so in the context of an action."[49] The concepts concerned fall into two main groups, the first concerned with efficiency, the second with correctness. Again, the concepts connected with

[47] Peters, *The Concept of Motivation,* pp. 5–6.
[48] *Ibid.,* p. 12.
[49] *Ibid.,* p. 14.

efficiency depend for their meaning primarily on the fact that actions are goal-directed. For, though actions are directed toward goals, we do not succeed in doing everything we set ourselves to do. Therefore we have some words whose job it is to attribute success or failure, like "murdered" or "flunked"; while others comment on choice of means, such as "intelligent" or "stupid." We say, for example, that Brutus murdered Caesar, meaning not only that Brutus stabbed Caesar with the intention of killing him but that he succeeded in carrying out his intention. Clearly, if a rock had fallen on Caesar and killed him we would not say that the rock murdered Caesar. The rock did not set itself the goal of killing anybody, and therefore it could neither succeed in doing so nor fail to do so. Again, when we say Johnny flunked, we use a word tailor-made to denote failure. One reason why we fail to do what we set out to do is because we don't go about it in the right way. Roses pruned too severely, for example, do not recover; if the intention is to produce bigger and better roses, therefore, severe pruning is not a very bright thing to do. We use what Ryle called "that family of . . . mental-conduct concepts . . . ordinarily surnamed 'intelligence'" to assess a person's choice of means for achieving his goals. When we do so we are concerned not with whether those goals were in fact achieved, but with whether the means relied upon to achieve them could reasonably have been expected to do so.

8. *Ascriptivism*

Both ends and means can also be appraised for what Peters calls their correctness. When we say that Brutus murdered Caesar, the use of the word "murdered" not only at-

tributes success to Brutus in his attempt to kill Caesar, it
also places the killing in a certain light. It was something
that ought not to have been done, since it broke a social
rule prohibiting actions of that sort. Brutus was therefore
responsible for Caesar's death, and if the social rule was a
rule of positive law he was legally as well as morally responsible.

To point out that action can be assessed in this way is to
draw attention to an important feature of the concept of action. Indeed, in "The Ascription of Responsibilities and
Rights,"[50] Professor H. L. A. Hart claimed that "the principal function . . . of sentences of the form 'He did it' is
what I venture to call ascriptive, being quite literally to
ascribe responsibility for actions" to individuals in accordance with "accepted rules of conduct"; just as "the principal
function of sentences of the form 'This is his' is to ascribe
rights in property." Sentences ascribing responsibility and
rights therefore share "logical peculiarities which distinguish
these kinds of sentences from descriptive sentences" that
"can best be grasped by considering certain characteristics
of legal concepts." A claim to a right under a contract, for
example, may be rejected if the "positive conditions required
for the existence of a valid contract, i.e., at least two *parties,*
an *offer* by one, *acceptance* by the other," etc., have not
been fulfilled. But "these conditions, although necessary,
are not always sufficient"; for even if satisfied, the claim
may be defeated by pointing to "other circumstances [that]
are present [and] which bring the case under some recog-
nised head of exception." The circumstances in which a
claim to a right under a contract may be defeated, even
though the positive conditions are satisfied, are "extremely
heterogeneous" and cannot be incorporated into any general

---

[50] Hart, "The Ascription of Responsibility and Rights." Hart ex-
cluded this article from a recently published collection of his essays
on the grounds that "its main contentions no longer seem to me de-
fensible." (*Punishment and Responsibility,* Preface.)

formula without distortion. Therefore Hart says that the concept of a contract is a *defeasible* concept.[51]

Hart's claim, then, is that "our concept of an action, like our concept of property, is a social concept and logically dependent on accepted rules of conduct. It is fundamentally not descriptive, but ascriptive in character; and it is a defeasible concept to be defined through exceptions and not by a set of necessary and sufficient conditions whether physical or physiological." Saying " 'Smith hit her,' " for example, "after observing the physical movements of a living person in conjunction with another . . . is an ascription of liability justified by the facts; for the observed physical movements of Smith's body are the circumstances which, in the absence of some defence, support, or are good reasons for the ascriptive sentence 'He did it.' " To regard "Smith hit her" as descriptive would be to make the mistake of "identifying the meaning of a non-descriptive utterance ascribing responsibility in stronger or weaker form, with the factual circumstances which support or are good reasons for the ascription."[52]

Although Hart's account is important both historically and for the points it makes, it cannot be accepted as a general account of the concept of action. We sometimes know that an action has been performed and describe it without ascribing responsibility in any sense to anyone, e.g., "Caesar was stabbed" or "The bed has been slept in." These sentences are not of the form "He did it"; rather they are of the form "It was done." Thus, though they are used to talk about actions, they provide no place that could be filled by an expression used to refer to an agent. Indeed, though if an action has been performed it must have been performed *by* someone, we sometimes use sentences of this form to talk about an action without knowing who performed it. We cannot therefore be using them to ascribe responsibility.

[51] *Ibid.*, pp. 171–89, *passim.*
[52] *Ibid.*, pp. 189–90, *passim.*

Moreover, as pointed out in Chapter I, there is an ambiguity in the word "responsibility" between "causally responsible as agent" and "morally or legally responsible"; and it is not clear in which sense Hart is using it.[53] We need to know who has performed an action—i.e., to ascribe causal responsibility to an agent—before there can be any question of ascribing moral or legal responsibility to anyone for it. "Brutus stabbed Caesar" or "Goldylocks slept in the bed" may be used to provide this information, telling us *who* stabbed Caesar or slept in the bed. Later the same sentences may be used to explain why Brutus is being executed or Goldylocks chased from the forest, now being used to ascribe moral or legal responsibility. Thus the use that is being made of a sentence (its illocutionary force) cannot be determined independently of the context in which it is used; indeed, in the context of a history lesson or a story, "Brutus stabbed Caesar" or "Goldylocks slept in the bed" may be used simply to describe what happened. Thus sentences of the form "He did it" may be used to describe what was done, to say who did it, or to ascribe moral or legal responsibility to the person who did it. And of these three uses, the descriptive use is primary; we ascribe responsibility *to* someone *for* what they do. Therefore before moral responsibility can be ascribed for an action, the action must be described and the agent identified. And the ascription of moral responsibility can be defeated either by challenging the description ("It wasn't like that") or denying the agency ("It wasn't me"), as well as by pleading extenuating circumstances ("I am a politician" or "I am a hippie").

In saying that the ascription of responsibility is the principal function of sentences of the form "He did it," Hart seems to have had in mind moral or legal responsibility. This is suggested by the analogy with contractual rights, the alleged dependence of the concept of action on accepted rules of

---

[53] Hart distinguishes four main senses of responsibility in Chapter IX of *Punishment and Responsibility*.

conduct, and the fact that such ascriptions give rise to liability against which defense may be needed. Hart is thinking, therefore, of the sense of "responsible" that is closely related to "obligation."

In *The Concept of Law* Hart points out that "the existence of social rules . . . making certain types of behaviour a standard, is the normal, though unstated, background" for a statement that a person has an obligation; and that "the distinctive function of such statement is to apply such a general rule to a particular person by calling attention to the fact that his case falls under it." And he points out that we use a "varied normative vocabulary ('ought,' 'must,' 'should') . . . to draw attention to the standard and to deviations from it."[54] Questions of responsibility, then, arise only when someone fails to meet his obligations, either by doing something that he ought not to have done or by failing to do something that he ought to have done—for example, when Brutus killed Caesar or Smith fell behind with his maintenance payments.

But not all actions are open to criticism in this way. If you are involved in a car crash and report it to the police you have done the right thing. Other actions are merely unconventional, such as wearing a Stetson in London or New York; we would not say that Smith was responsible for wearing a Stetson in New York unless, perhaps, he caused a riot. More important, most actions are neither prohibited nor required by social rules, whether moral, legal, or conventional; and therefore though we may be interested in what people do, we have no occasion to assess their actions in any way. To say that Smith made himself a cup of coffee or went for a walk in the park is simply to say that that is what he did; no question of responsibility arises. In talking about defeasibility Hart is drawing attention to our willingness to qualify descriptions of actions in ways that affect the extent to which they attract praise or blame; but most descriptions of actions contain no hint of the need for adverbial qualification of this sort. He is therefore giving an account of the appraisal of actions for their correctness and can be regarded as elaborating on the rule-following purposive model of action rather than offering an independent general account of the concept of action.

Actions then may be appraised for their efficiency or their correctness. We make such assessments both *ex post*—after the action has been performed—and *ex ante*—before the action has been performed. In both cases the appraisals made could be expressed using the word "ought," though it would perhaps be more natural to talk of responsibility in the case of *ex post* assessments. At any rate this is the use of "ought" that is stressed in moral theories that regard moral discourse as primarily having the practical function of guiding actions. If you want lots of roses, for example, you ought to leave lots of buds on the rose trees when pruning them. Here the advice is hypothetical; if you don't want lots of roses there is no reason why you should follow it. Advice about the correctness of proposed actions is more often categorical. You ought not to kill your maiden aunt, however much you stand to gain under her will. The possibility of saying that an action ought or ought not to be done, however, depends on the possibility of *describing* that action, just as the possibility of saying that Brutus was (morally) responsible for Caesar's death depends on the possibility of saying that Brutus killed Caesar. Therefore if we wish to consider the question of whether there is a logical gap between the language of actions and the language of physical movement, the relevant comparison is between descriptions of actions and descriptions of physical movements. The logical gap that results when *assessments* of actions are compared with *descriptions* of physical movements is that between assessment and description. The existence of this logical gap is grounds for claiming that there is a logical gap between action and physical movement only if physical movements cannot be assessed for their efficiency and correctness in the same way as actions. Therefore, too much reliance cannot be placed on examples like "Brutus murdered Caesar" in which what Brutus did is both described and assessed. Much more of the language of action is ambiguous in this way than appears at first sight; but the case against physicalism cannot rest on this fact alone.

9. The Possibility of a Physicalist Account of Intentions

I have considered only the main outlines of the rule-following purposive model of action. There are many important details to be filled in, and a great deal of recent work has been directed to this end. In a well-known article called "A Plea for Excuses," J. L. Austin discussed the topic of excuses—the different ways in which, in Hart's terminology, an ascription of responsibility could be defeated. And in "Three Ways of Spilling Ink" he distinguished carefully between acting *intentionally*, *deliberately*, and *on purpose*.[55] Indeed, Austin's view was that an investigation of these topics was not simply a matter of filling in details, the broad outline being already understood; on the contrary, "to examine excuses is to examine cases where there has been some abnormality or failure: and as so often, the abnormality will throw light on the normal, will help us to penetrate the blinding veil of ease and obviousness that hides the mechanisms of the natural successful act."[56] In this section, however, I will consider only the claim that the

[55] Austin, *Philosophical Papers*. "A Plea for Excuses" was originally published in *Proceedings of the Aristotelian Society* in 1956–57 and is also reprinted in *Ordinary Language*, edited by V. C. Chappell, and in *The Philosophy of Action*, edited by Alan R. White.

[56] *Ibid.*, pp. 127–28.

principal features of the purposive rule-following model of action rules out a physicalist account of action in terms of bodily movement.

Peters' arguments were directed not against the physicalist position that I have outlined but against ambitious, all-embracing psychological theories of human behavior, especially that of C. L. Hull and his followers; and a great deal of his detailed argument is very much to the point. Nevertheless, his main contention—that an account of action in terms of bodily movement is ruled out—is not as easily sustained against physicalism when developed by a philosopher such as Smart as when directed at the philosophical *obiter dicta* of professional psychologists. In being redirected in this way it gains in one way; it is no longer open to the accusation of saying, on a priori grounds, that psychologists cannot provide causal explanations of genuine behavior when in fact they have already had some success in doing so. Indeed, it is the physicalist who is now open to the charge of a priorism in appearing to deny the obvious fact of consciousness as a mode of happening distinct from physical happening.

Peters said that *"his* reason," i.e., the reason a man gives, or would give if he were honest, for what he does ". . . entails that a man is conscious of his objective."[57] He does not explicitly stress consciousness but would obviously agree with Hamlyn that the application of the "conceptual scheme which centers round the concept of action"[58] presupposes consciousness. I have already discussed and rejected Smart's claim that a physicalist account of consciousness is possible. Here I will assume that Hamlyn is correct in saying that action concepts presuppose consciousness and will introduce a second set of concepts differing from the original ones only in that this presupposition is withdrawn. If this withdrawal is indicated by the subscript "c," then corresponding

---

[57] Peters, *The Concept of Motivation*, p. 9.
[58] Hamlyn, "Causality and Human Behavior," *Supplement, Proceedings of the Aristotelian Society*, XXXVIII, 1964, p. 138.

to "action," "intention," "purpose," "goal," "rule-following," and "movement" we get "action$_c$," "intention$_c$," "purpose$_c$," "rule-following$_c$," "movement$_c$," and so on. The question I will consider is whether a physicalist account of the latter concepts is possible.

Smart, replying to Hamlyn on "Causality and Human Behaviour," claims that "what is important in intention is not consciousness but goal-directedness." Goal-directedness is indeed the crux of Peters' account of action; but Smart claims that it is possible to give a physicalist account of it. Machines such as "a fully automatic aeroplane with goal-seeking navigating equipment built into it," could, he argues, display goal-directed behavior and, therefore, be said to perform actions$_c$, even if not actions. Such a plane would vary the movements$_c$ it made to reach, say, the North Pole in accordance with varying circumstances. If driven off course by a severe storm over Greenland, it would plot a new course and eventually reach its destination just the same. If it failed to reach the North Pole and arrived in London instead, it could still be said to have intended$_c$ to reach the North Pole but unintentionally$_c$ arrived at London instead. "A mechanist," Smart concludes, "can therefore distinguish between an action (something done intentionally or unintentionally) and a mere set of bodily movements as such."[59] Reference to intentions or goal-directedness could, indeed, be eliminated from the physicalist account altogether in favor of descriptions of the physical state of the plane and its physical environment and a complex sequence of interactions between them.

It is also clear that the plane's performance could be described as intelligent$_c$ as opposed to mechanical in a derogatory sense; it could also, therefore, be described as stupid$_c$. (I will leave out the subscript "c" from now on; it is in any case often debatable which concepts require it.) Smart can therefore agree with Peters that "movements *qua* movements

[59] Smart, "Causality and Human Behavior," pp. 147–48.

are neither intelligent, efficient or correct. They only become so in the context of an action."[60] If it is appropriate to speak of the plane as having a goal and as taking steps to reach it, then it is also appropriate to assess the steps taken for their efficiency or inefficiency.

It might be objected, however, that though the plane displays the appearance of purpose, its behavior is not in fact purposive. It behaves as though it had a goal, but it does not in fact have one. This is not merely because the plane is unaware of the goal toward which its movements are directed, but because Smart's story lacks anything corresponding to the adoption of the North Pole as the destination of the plane's journey. It did not choose to go there and it would not make sense to say either that it wanted or did not want to go there. Nor would it make sense to say that it was glad to get there or would have been disappointed if it had failed to do so. It simply moved in the direction of the North Pole because someone decided that it should and set the controls accordingly.

These objections are fairly easy to deal with. The automatic pilot and navigator of such a plane are artifacts that replace men in some of their functions, not all of them.[61] But there is no reason why a machine capable of choosing its own goals should not be constructed. A mechanical "tortoise" was constructed by Gray Walter some years ago that was powered by electricity and programmed to seek out electric power sources when its batteries were running low. Therefore it could be said to have a built-in disposition to seek out certain goals and direct its own activity toward their achievement. And the physical state that gives rise to that disposition could obviously be described wholly in physical terms. The tortoise was of course programmed by its inventor, and its choice of goals was restricted and its behavior patterns limited. But though animals and men are

---

[60] Peters, *The Concept of Motivation*, p. 14.
[61] Smart, *Philosophy and Scientific Realism*, pp. 108-9.

not programmed, they do inherit a genetic constitution that functions in the same way. They display a wide choice of goals and are flexible in the means they adopt to achieve them. Of course, behavior differs enormously in complexity from one end of the phylogenetic scale to the other. Even more important, it differs in the extent to which it exhibits novelty in adopting new goals and in using new ways to achieve them. The ability to learn, or plasticity, is for many psychologists the most important feature of organic life. And though the mechanical tortoise did not display this feature, there is no reason why artifacts that do cannot be constructed. For example, the automatic plane might be built in such a way that it could cope with navigational hazards of a sort that had not been foreseen by its makers. It might also, on finding no suitable landing site at the North Pole, adopt a new goal, seeking out a more interesting location, such as London or New York.

It might also be possible to find an application for concepts like disappointment or frustration on failing to achieve a goal. A machine that is directing its behavior toward the achievement of a goal may prepare responses appropriate to its intended situation. It may, for example, check its de-icing equipment. In failing to reach the goal, however, it does not come to occupy a situation in which those responses are appropriate. An inappropriate production of the response may then be the best way of restoring the status quo; and such responses could be described as expressions of frustration or disappointment.

There is no reason then why performances describable wholly in physical language should not be assessed for their efficiency. Even the adoption of new goals can be assessed as intelligent or stupid by reference to the long-term interest of the mechanism concerned. An intelligent plane, for example, will seek out refueling bases on its way to the Pole, just as the members of a polar expedition will lay down caches of food to make sure they do not starve to death. A stupid plane will head directly for the Pole and run out of fuel in consequence. The logical gap between description and assessment remains, but does not have the implications for "action" claimed for it.

Similar considerations apply to the second feature of Peters' account of action, its stress on social rules and the consequent possibility of assessing actions for their correctness using normative concepts logically distinct from those used to describe. Smart agrees that "an isolated machine could not sign a document, because the notion of signing presupposes a set of legal and sociological rules." But if a group of machines could communicate and "had evolved, or perhaps had built into them, a set of rules of behaviour and a legal terminology . . . such machines could correctly be said to sign documents."[62] To argue in this way is to admit that what such machines did could not be described using only physical concepts, but only because a covert assessment is incorporated into the description. There is indeed no a priori reason why artifacts should not be said to sign documents—provided we are also prepared to apply to them, without reservation, the rest of the language of action and social activity that at present we apply only to people. In doing this we would no longer be looking on them merely as mechanisms; and we would be no more justified in discriminating against them merely because they were made of metal or silicon than we are at present justified in discriminating against other human beings merely because the color of their skin differs from our own. I think that this line of speculation has reached the limit of its usefulness. What is really required is a detailed explication of the language of social activity. Without this it is not clear what we would be doing in accepting such machines as social beings like ourselves.

A final objection to the possibility of a physicalist account of intentions is that people are in a privileged position regarding knowledge of their own intentions, and therefore

[62] *Ibid.*, p. 110.

of their own actions. Others see only the physical movements that are made; and though from these they may infer
the agent's intention, they are always liable to error; for
identical movements may be made with different intentions,
and only the person himself knows what his intentions are.
If, however, intentions$_c$ are considered, thus withdrawing
any implication of consciousness from the use of the word
"intention," a person's privileged knowledge of his own intentions can be accounted for by a self-scanning mechanism
within the brain. Self-knowledge is then only contingently
privileged; any qualified electronics engineer, for example,
could discover the automatic plane's intentions by examin-
ing the present state of its computer banks. But there is no
reason why a physicalist should resist this conclusion.

CHAPTER IV

Persons and Agents

1. Actions and Those Who Perform Them

In Chapter I I contrasted causal and moral responsibility and went on to distinguish two senses of causal responsibility—the sense in which the rain (strictly, the rainfall) was responsible, as cause, for the landslide and the sense in which Brutus was responsible, as agent, for Caesar's death. And I suggested that the notion of responsibility as agent, or agency, cannot be reduced to the notion of causal responsibility, since "Brutus" in "Brutus killed Caesar" could not be replaced without loss of meaning by a description of a physical or mental event.

According to Prichard, the analysis of "Brutus killed Caesar" would be roughly—

1. A special kind of mental event called a volition was causally responsible for a movement of a human body, which in turn was causally responsible for a movement of a dagger, which in turn caused Caesar's death; and

2. the mental event was part of a series of mental events that occurred in Brutus' mind.

According to Smart, the analysis of "Brutus killed Caesar" would be roughly—

1. A brain event was causally responsible for a movement of a human body, which in turn was causally responsible for a movement of a dagger, which in turn caused Caesar's death; and

2. the brain event and the bodily movement caused by it occurred in the physicochemical body we call Brutus.

Insofar as the notion of a person occurs in these analyses, persons are thought of as minds in which mental events occur or as complex physicochemical bodies; in neither case does the notion of agency occur. This is clearly so in Smart's case. In Prichard's case the special mental activity of "setting myself to do" or "willing" is described as an activity that *we* perform; therefore it might be suggested with some plausibility that the notion of agency is contained in that of volition. But if so, then Prichard is taking for granted the main feature of what he set out to elucidate; perhaps this is why his complicated maneuvers achieve so little.

Agency is of central importance for the concept of action. We attribute agency to people, not to events or things. To some extent this is reflected in the grammatical form of the sentences that we use to talk about the actions that people perform. For example, we use an active form of verb to indicate agency—"Brutus stabbed Caesar" attributes agency to Brutus. But we also use grammatically similar sentences when talking about physical events without intending to attribute agency—when, for example, we say that the fallen rocks blocked the road. What is important therefore is the difference in logical, not grammatical, form between sentences that report the occurrence of actions and those that report the occurrence of other events.

Of a purported action it will always make sense to ask "Who did it?"; an action must be performed by, or ascribable to, someone. To say that nobody did it is to deny that it was an action at all. For example, to say that nobody destroyed Pompeii is not to deny that Pompeii was destroyed but to deny that the destruction of Pompeii by the eruption of Mount Vesuvius counts as an action. We sometimes know that an action has been performed without knowing who performed it; the police investigating a murder are often in this position. People do die of natural causes, but a knife in the back is not one of them. Similarly, flowers grow wild in the hedgerows, but only in orderly gardens if tended by a gardener. If Caesar was knifed in the back or the flowers neatly staked and the flower beds weeded someone must, logically, have knifed Caesar in the back or staked the flowers and weeded the flower beds; it could not be true that Caesar was knifed in the back and false that someone knifed Caesar. Our interest in an action need not lead us to look for the person who performed it. We may say that the west door of the cathedral was intricately carved, making no explicit reference to the man who did the carving. But we know from experience that wood does not naturally assume that form and, therefore, that somebody must have done the carving. It would make sense to ask who did the carving, even though we might not wish to do so in a particular case.

The statement that we attribute agency only to people and never to events or things is not strictly true as an account of the way we actually speak. We say, for example, that the car refuses to start; and we may shout at, or even strike, the table leg against which we have stubbed our toe when walking barefoot. If pressed, we might agree that the car did not refuse to start but merely failed to do so; and that the only result of hitting the table is likely to be a bruised hand as well as a bruised toe. In ancient Greece, however, inanimate objects that had accidentally killed a man were destroyed; while in the Middle Ages animals were sometimes punished, hence the expression "hang-dog." This attitude was reflected later in the old English law of homicide, according to which an object that was responsible for the death of a man became a "deodand," i.e., was given to God in order to purge its guilt; it was not destroyed but sold, the money being used for prayer.[1] So there is an element of stipulation in insisting that we attribute agency only to people; but it is a stipulation that I do not hesitate to make.

In order to understand the concept of action, therefore, we need to look at those who perform actions, that is, at agents. We cannot, however, point to anyone who is simply an agent; all we can point to are people. People—Jones who crossed the road to buy some tobacco, Smith who hit her, Brutus who killed Caesar, and the rest—are agents; but they are not merely agents. What else do people do besides perform actions; and how are the other things that they do related to what they do as agents? To try to throw some light on these questions I will look briefly at the concept of a person.

2. Persons

Professor Strawson's aim in *Individuals* is to "describe the actual structure of our thought about the world" and "to exhibit some general and structural features of the conceptual scheme in terms of which we think about particular things."[2] By "particular things" (or "particulars") he means, very roughly, the things we talk to each other about when, for example, we say that Thomas the cat is washing his face. Communication is possible only if one person knows what another is talking about, i.e., can identify the particular thing—in this case Thomas the cat—which is the subject

[1] Kenney, *Outlines of Criminal Law,* pp. 35 and 106–7. I owe this reference to Professor O'Connor.
[2] Strawson, *Individuals,* pp. 9 and 15.

of the other's remarks. All the things we succeed in talking about can, he says, be located within a single, unified, spatiotemporal system of relations. Using that system we build for ourselves a unified picture of the world "in which we ourselves have a place, and in which every element is thought of as directly or indirectly related to every other. . . . By means of identifying references, we fit other people's reports and stories, along with our own, into the single story about empirical reality."[3]

We can identify some things directly, if necessarily demonstratively, by pointing to them or touching them; these Strawson calls "basic particulars." The basic particulars are material bodies and those things that possess material bodies, i.e., persons. Material bodies are "three-dimensional objects with some endurance through time"; they, and only they, are therefore able to confer on the spatiotemporal framework "its own fundamental characteristics."[4] We also succeed in talking about things that are not basic particulars, identifying them indirectly by means of their relation to a material body that can be identified directly. For example, we can talk about what Strawson calls "private particulars" such as the pain that Caesar felt when stabbed by Brutus because we can identify the pain as that of Caesar; and Caesar, since he possesses a body, can be directly located within the spatiotemporal framework.

What is most relevant in this account is the central place in our conceptual scheme accorded to persons. Persons can be identified directly through their bodies and are therefore basic particulars; but they are not identified with their bodies. Strawson defines the concept of a person in terms of the sorts of predicates that it attracts. "The concept of a person is the concept of a type of entity such that *both* predicates ascribing states of consciousness *and* predicates ascribing corporeal characteristics, a physical situation, etc.,

[3] *Ibid.*, p. 29.
[4] *Ibid.*, p. 39.

are equally applicable to a single individual of that single type."[5] Persons are neither complex physicochemical bodies, as suggested by Smart, nor collections of mental events, as Prichard supposed, nor any sort of combination of a body and a mind. Indeed, it is only because we have the concept of a person that we can also speak of a person's body and of a person's mind. Strawson introduced the term M-predicate to refer to predicates ascribing corporeal characteristics and P-predicate to refer to predicates ascribing states of consciousness. "Though not all P-predicates are what we should call 'predicates ascribing states of consciousness' (e.g., 'going for a walk' is not), they may be said to have this in common, that they imply the possession of consciousness on the part of that to which they are ascribed."[6]

If the basic outlines of Strawson's account of our conceptual scheme are correct, it follows that we cannot eliminate references to persons from our talk about the world without also eliminating references to states of consciousness or mental events. Therefore sentences of the form "Brutus killed Caesar" cannot be analyzed in the way attributed to Prichard at the beginning of this chapter, or in any similar manner. The objection to such analyses is not simply that they result in loss of meaning or depart from the way we normally talk without adequate justification, but that the proposed way of talking is not independently viable as a way of talking. Indeed, it can only be expressed in terms of the conceptual scheme that it proposes to replace, since both the mental event that causes a movement of a human body and the human body that is caused to move are assumed to belong to the same person, i.e., Brutus.[7]

It would be more convenient for my purpose to depart slightly from Strawson's account and define a person as one who possesses the sort of conceptual scheme that Strawson

[5] *Ibid.*, pp. 101–2.

[6] *Ibid.*, p. 105.

[7] See Strawson's arguments against the no-ownership theory in *Individuals*, pp. 95–98.

describes. The possession and use of such a scheme provides a link between the two sorts of consciousness that I distinguished earlier—the awareness of relevant features of the environment that is displayed in behavior, with which Smart was primarily concerned; and the consciousness that, in Hamlyn's view, accompanies such awareness. We can be aware of, or conscious of, only those features of the world that have a place in our conceptual scheme. Using that scheme, we are able to recognize particular things as being of a certain sort, having recognizable properties, and spatially related to one another in determinate ways. We note also that some things cease to exist while others come into existence and that changes occur in the properties and position of those things that continue to exist. Therefore our picture of the way things are in the world is subject to constant modification. Though the possibility of our conceptual scheme depends on the existence of "three-dimensional objects with some endurance through time,"[8] our conception of the world is a conception of a world in which change is constantly taking place in a reasonably ordered way, i.e., in which events occur. So, although material objects are, according to Strawson, the basic particulars from the point of view of identification, events also form an important class of particulars in our conceptual scheme.

Equally important from the present point of view is the concept of a person, the second sort of basic particular. In possessing a conceptual scheme in which the concept of a person is itself a basic particular, persons recognize both themselves and others as persons and, therefore, as persons living in communities of persons. The relations between persons in such communities are social relations that differ logically from relations between material things; therefore our conceptual scheme allows for relations such as those that exist between father and son, customer and shopkeeper,

[8] *Ibid.*, p. 39.

and worker and manager, as well as between those who feel compassion, love, or hate and the objects of their feelings. Finally, our conceptual scheme allows us to see ourselves and others not merely as passive observers in a world of change but, on occasion, as instrumental in bringing about change—that is to say, it includes the concept of action. Of particular importance are those actions which, directly or indirectly, affect other persons and not merely things, and which are therefore the subject of social control via public rules reflecting the concept of a person as a subject of respect. The consequent possibility of assessing actions by reference to such rules was discussed in Section 8 of the previous chapter.

3. *Observers and Agents*

I want now to consider in more detail how the possession of the conceptual scheme in terms of which the concept of a person has been defined shows itself.

First, a distinction can be made between what people do and what happens to them. M-predicates ascribing bodily features can be ascribed to persons as well as to material bodies; and the sorts of things that happen to material bodies can happen also to persons. For example, their bodies can enter into physical interaction with other physical bodies, as happened when the rock fell from the cliff and hit Brutus' arm. Some of the things that happen to persons could not, however, also happen to physical bodies; their occurrence is therefore reported by the use of a P-predicate. Caesar, for example, was assassinated, not merely killed as a plant or an insect might be killed; and being assassinated is something that can, logically, happen only to a person and, probably, a person occupying a particular political role. The

language of emotion is largely concerned with people's reactions to the things that happen to them; Caesar's words
"et tu, Brute," express his sadness at such treatment from
one thought of as a friend. Other things that happen to
persons are intermediate between these two cases. Suffering
pain is something that happens to a person rather than
something that they do; but we normally suppose that other
living creatures whom we would not regard as persons also
suffer pain. It is not clear therefore whether suffering pain
is something that can happen to persons only because of
their ability to ascribe to themselves and others the predicate
"is in pain." But it is what people do, rather than what happens to them, that is relevant here, so I need not consider
this question further.

The most important thing people do besides performing
actions is make observations. Those who make observations
may be called observers, as those who perform actions were
called agents. An observer is a person thought of as one who
judges, or observes, that something is the case, and so comes
to believe that something is the case. In the past philosophers have thought of persons primarily as observers; this is
reflected in the central importance attached to perception
as the source of knowledge by the classical empiricist philosophers. To some extent the position has now changed,
a change reflected in the contrast between Wittgenstein's
Tractatus and the posthumously published *Philosophical
Investigations*. We who, in *Tractatus* 2.1, "picture facts
to ourselves" are observers; and the metaphysical subject who
"does not belong to the world" is simply the point of view
from which we observe how things are in the world. In the
Investigations people are no longer thought of merely as
observers; they take part in language-games, which consist
of both "language and the actions into which it is woven,"[9]
and their use of language can be understood only by un-

---

[9] Wittgenstein, *Tractatus Logico-Philosophicus*, 5.632, and *Philosophical Investigations*, I, 7.

derstanding the part that it plays in the complete language game. As long as persons were thought of primarily as observers, it was natural also to think of language as used only to describe what was observed. Wittgenstein, however, drew attention, by means of carefully developed examples, to the many different ways in which people use words in different parts of the language games they play. In those games, people are not simply passive observers of the way things are in the world, but are actively engaged, in co-operation with others, in changing things; buying and selling, fetching and carrying, using tools and building, and so on. Observation, and the related use of words as the names of things, plays a part in such activities, but alongside and interrelated with the rest of the activity. The words "five red apples" may be used as part of the activity of shopping, the words "slab," "beam," and "pillar" as part of the activity of building.

The importance of agency and the interdependence of action and observation are explicitly stressed by Professor Hampshire in his book *Thought and Action*. "The deepest mistake in empiricist theories of perception, descending from Berkeley and Hume," he says, "has been the representation of human beings as passive observers receiving impressions from 'outside' of the mind, where the 'outside' includes their own bodies. In fact I find myself from the beginning able to act upon objects around me." "We are in the world, as bodies among bodies, not only as observers but as active experimenters. We could not ever be observers unless we were sometimes active experimenters, and we could not ever be experimenters unless we were sometimes observers."[10]

The philosophers who thought of persons primarily as observers tended also to think of perception as wholly passive; but this too is mistaken. Perceptual experience is structured by the conceptual scheme which, as persons, we

[10] Hampshire, *Thought and Action,* pp. 47 and 53.

apply to the world; and there is psychological evidence that, within the limits imposed by our concepts, attention is highly selective. Even at a conscious level, perception is not always passive. Our senses frequently provide us with information about the world for which we have been actively seeking; we may, for example, have been looking everywhere for the cat when we see it on the candelabra. It is true that they also give us information for which we have not been seeking, some of which may be positively unwelcome; we may hear the cat courting on the garden wall long after we would have wished to have been asleep. Verbs of perception, therefore, have both an active and a passive form—looking at and seeing, listening to and hearing, touching and feeling, etc. We look closely at a piece of silver to see the hallmark; we see a car being driven down the street without taking much notice of it. We see the ball game because we intended to see it, but hear the cat on the garden wall despite our intention of getting a good night's sleep.

The things that people do intentionally, therefore, include what they do as observers as well as what they do as agents. So action cannot be distinguished from observation by the presence of intention in the case of action, and by its absence in the case of observation. Indeed, in both cases the presence of intention is a matter of degree; some intentions are consciously and explicitly formulated, while others are ill-defined and hardly recognized by the person whose intention they are. In both cases there is a continuum from what might be called full-blown cases to those that are little more than reflexes. But the intentions with which people do things are of two main sorts—observations are made with the intention of discovering the way things are in the world; actions are performed with the intention of changing the way things are in the world. Even when observations are made intentionally, the distinction between observation and action, and therefore between ob-

servers and agents, can be maintained by means of this
difference in intention.

At this point it is worth considering the role that bodily
movements play in action and observation, respectively. It is
commonly assumed that bodily movement is necessarily involved in action but that, by contrast, it need not be involved in observation and, as a matter of fact, usually is not.
I suggest that bodily movement is not necessary for either
action or observation but that usually, perhaps always, it is
involved in both. Gross bodily movement is frequently part
of the process of observation. This is least obvious in the
case of vision; but the content of the visual field depends
partly on our location, and we frequently change our location in order to see what we want to see. And in all cases
seeing involves eye movement; if the retinal image is
stabilized by the use of experimental techniques, it quickly
disappears. Similarly, what we hear depends on where we
are, and we frequently move nearer to the source of sounds
that we wish to hear more clearly. Touch and taste involve
bodily contact, and this is normally achieved by means of
bodily movement; and continued tactile observation requires continued movement, as for example in reading
Braille. And of course we go into the garden in the late evening to smell the honeysuckle, and breathe deeply in order
to do so. It does not follow from the fact of bodily movement, therefore, that what someone is doing is acting rather
than observing. Someone stroking a cat, for example, may be
doing so in order to make the cat purr; but he may be also
doing so in order to assess the commercial value of its pelt.

Turning now to actions, it might be argued that it is a
contingent matter that we need to move our bodies in order
to effect changes in the world. We understand what is
meant by psychokinesis even if, at best, it occurs only rarely
and on a limited scale. Indeed, there is no obvious contradic-
tion in supposing that God is active in the world but lacks
a body. These examples might be thought to be question
begging. But it is clear that no movement of the agent's body

is involved in what are sometimes called acts of omission. In such acts people refrain from a positive action that they would normally perform or that they would be convention- ally expected to perform in the circumstances—for example, suspending family planning measures in order to start a family or failing to do what was necessary to keep a newly born but deformed child alive. The changes that result from such acts—the beginning of a family or the death of the child—are foreseen by the agent, and the act of omission is performed in order to bring them about. They are there- fore actions, despite the absence of bodily movement on the part of the agent; and people are often held morally, and sometimes legally, responsible for such actions. It is clear of course that there could be no acts of omission unless there were also actions of the sort that, by contrast, I have called positive actions.

I want to consider now those actions that are performed by the use of words and that involve no more in the way of bodily movement than is involved in the use of words. The use of words does, of course, involve movements of the tongue, lips, and larynx; but the role of such movements in speech is no greater than that played by eye movements in visual perception. This class of actions is sufficiently im- portant to receive separate consideration in the next section.

4. *Doing Things with Words*

In an important article called "Other Minds," Professor J. L. Austin pointed out that, though I can say "I believe p (though I may be wrong)" and "I hope to do A (but I may not)," to say "I know" or "I promise" is "taking a new plunge. But it is *not* saying 'I have performed a specially striking feat of cognition, superior, in the same scale as be-

lieving and feeling sure.'" When I say "I promise," "I have
not merely announced my intention, but, by using this
formula (performing this ritual), I have bound myself to
others, and staked my reputation, in a new way." Similarly,
"when I say 'I know,' I give others my word: I give others
my authority for saying 'S is P.'"[11] And later he added,
"To suppose that 'I know' is a descriptive phrase, is only one
example of the descriptive fallacy, so common in philosophy. . . . Utterance of obvious ritual phrases, in the appropriate circumstances, is not *describing* the action we are
doing, but doing it."[12] Austin called such utterances "performatives" and contrasted them with declarative or, as he
preferred to call them, "constative" utterances. In a later
article, "Performative-Constative," he said, "The constative
utterance under the name, so dear to philosophers, of *statement,* has the property of being true or false. The performative utterance, by contrast, can never be either: it has its
own special job, it is used to perform an action. To issue
such an utterance *is* to perform the action—an action, perhaps, which one scarcely could perform, at least with so
much precision, in any other way. Here are some examples:

> I name this ship 'Liberté.'
>
> I apologise.
>
> I welcome you.
>
> I advise you to do it."[13]

And in *How to Do Things with Words,* he said ". . . the
issuing of the utterance is the performance of an action—
it is not normally thought of as just saying something."[14]

Austin is making two important points here. First, he is
pointing out that we use language not only to describe what
we observe but also in other ways; to suppose we are using

[11] Austin, *Philosophical Papers,* p. 67.

[12] *Ibid.,* p. 71.

[13] Austin, "Performative-Constative." This article was originally
published as "Performatif-Constatif" in *La Philosophie Analytique,*
Paris, 1962.

[14] ———, *How to Do Things with Words,* p. 6.

language descriptively when we are using it in one of the other ways is to commit what he calls the descriptive fallacy. I suggested in the previous section that the assumption that language is used only to describe what is observed is a consequence of thinking of people primarily as passive observers. Second, Austin is pointing to one of the other ways in which we do use language: we use language in order to perform actions. In making this point, therefore, Austin is implicitly recognizing the fact that people are agents as well as observers. It follows also that when actions are performed by means of words, the only bodily movements that need be involved are those by means of which the words are given perceptible form.

I think Austin was correct in claiming that we can use language in order to perform actions. However, the account that I have given so far is oversimplified; moreover, Austin himself later expressed doubts as to whether the distinction between performative and constative utterances could be maintained. Even in the original "Other Minds" article Austin recognized that the mere utterance of a linguistic formula is insufficient. "In these 'ritual' cases, the approved case is one where *in the appropriate circumstances,* I say a certain formula: e.g., 'I do' when standing, unmarried or a widower, beside a woman, unmarried or a widow and not within the prohibited degrees of relationship, before a clergyman, registrar, etc., or 'I give' when it is mine to give, etc., or 'I order' when I have authority to, etc. But now, if the situation transpires to have been in some way not orthodox (I was already married; it wasn't mine to give; I had no authority to order), then we tend to be rather hesitant about how to put it, as heaven was when the saint blessed the penguins."[15] Thus "besides the utterance of the so-called performative, a good many other things have as a general rule to be right and to go right if we are to be said to have happily brought off our action."[16]

[15] Austin, *Philosophical Papers,* p. 70.
[16] ———, *How to Do Things with Words,* p. 14.

Later, however, Austin realized that constatives also can "fail to get by in more than one way"[17] and that some of the ways in which they fail to get by correspond to ways in which performatives can be unhappy. First, saying "All John's children are bald" (and equally "All John's children are not bald") presupposes that John has children. But John may have no children. Similarly, saying "I bequeath my watch to you" presupposes that I have a watch. But I may not have a watch. Second, saying "The cat is on the mat" (though not "The cat is not on the mat") implies that I believe it is. But I may not believe it is. Similarly, saying "I promise to meet you" implies that I intend to be there. But I may not intend to be there. Third, saying "All the guests are French" entails that it is false that some of the guests are not French. But I may go on to say "But some aren't." Similarly, in saying "I welcome you" I commit myself to treating you in a certain way, i.e., as a friend. But I may go on to treat you as an enemy. Austin therefore concluded that "the constative utterance is every bit as liable to unhappiness as the performative, and indeed to pretty much the same unhappinesses."[18]

Despite these points of comparison, it remains true that constative utterances may be true or false, whereas performatives cannot. But, Austin points out, performatives also are subject to "quasi-objective evaluation"[19]; advice may be criticized as good or bad, verdicts may be just or unjust, reprimands may be deserved or undeserved. Thus there is in the case of performatives "a confrontation of my utterance with the situation in, and the situation with respect to which, it was issued"[20] analogous to the confrontation of a constative with the facts on which its truth or falsity depends.

Finally, Austin asks "whether issuing a constative utter-

17 Austin, "Performative-Constative."
18 *Ibid.*, p. 29.
19 *Ibid.*, p. 32.
20 *Ibid.*, p. 31.

ance is not, after all, the performance of an act, the act, namely, of stating. Is stating an act in the same sense as marrying, apologising, betting, etc.?"[21] Clearly the answer to this question depends on the sense of "performance of an act" that is involved; and Austin considered this question in some detail in *How to Do Things with Words*. To say something is, first, always to perform a locutionary act, i.e., "the act of uttering certain noises . . . belonging to *and as* belong to a certain vocabulary . . . [having] a certain more or less definite 'sense' and a more or less definite 'reference.' "[22] Second, "to perform a locutionary act is in general . . . also and *eo ipso* to perform an *illocutionary* act. . . . To determine what illocutionary act is so performed we must determine in what way we are using the locution." Then follows a selection of examples of the "very numerous functions of or ways in which we use speech," i.e., of what Austin calls "illocutionary forces," which includes the following:

"asking or answering a question,

giving some information or an assurance or a warning,

announcing a verdict or an intention, . . .

making an identification or giving a description,

and the numerous like." Finally, performing the locutionary act of saying "Shoot her," and thereby also performing the illocutionary act of urging someone to shoot her, may also have the actual consequence of getting someone to shoot her. Then getting someone to shoot her is an example of what Austin called a perlocutionary act.[23]

Thus both performative and constative utterances are both locutionary and illocutionary acts, and may also be perlocutionary acts; they differ only in their illocutionary force. For, says Austin, "surely to state is every bit as much

21 *Ibid.*, p. 30.
22 Austin, *How to Do Things with Words,* pp. 92–93.
23 *Ibid.*, pp. 98–99.

to perform an illocutionary act as, say, to warn or to pronounce. . . . Consider such an unexceptionable remark as the following:

> In saying that it was raining, I was not betting or arguing or warning: I was simply stating it as a fact.

Here 'stating' is put absolutely on a level with arguing, betting, and warning."[24] It seems, therefore, that saying anything whatsoever is performing an action, and that there is no special sense in which performative utterances are actions.

But, while it is clear that to use language for any purpose is in some very general sense to do something, and, indeed, to do something intentionally, it is not also, necessarily, to perform an action unless the notion of an action is extended to include anything that a person may be said to do. It would of course be possible to stipulate that the concept of action be used in this way, but it is appropriate in philosophy to draw distinctions wherever there are proper grounds for doing so. In discussing observers and agents in the previous section, I suggested that observations are performed with the intention of discovering the way things are in the world, whereas actions are performed with the intention of changing the ways things are in the world. Similarly, language may be used in order to describe what is observed in the world or with the intention of changing the way things are in the world. I suggest that only when language is used in order to bring about change is an action performed. It might be argued that the making of observations brings about changes in the observer's beliefs and that descriptions of what is observed are made in order to change the beliefs of others. One who observes that the cat is on the mat or hears someone else state that the cat is on the mat may come to believe that the cat is on the mat and thereby acquire a belief that he did not possess before. But such changes are internal to the person's status

[24] *Ibid.,* p. 133.

as an observer; the subject of observation or description, the cat, remains unchanged by being observed; and it would not have remained unchanged if it had been the subject of an action. Assuming therefore that Austin's original distinction between performative and constative utterances can be maintained as a distinction between the kinds of illocutionary force, I now want to consider what can be done—which actions can be performed—with words.

I will confine myself to two cases: things that clearly cannot and things that clearly can be done with words. What you cannot change by means of words are the physical facts; you cannot, for example, move mountains or change people into toads. You can move mountains using dynamite or a bulldozer or some other physical means; it is physically impossible to change a person into a toad. People have thought that you could change people into toads by means of words; this suggests that our inability to bring about physical changes by means of words is a contingent feature of the world we live in. What you can change by means of words is your own or someone else's social, legal, or moral status or state. You can, if you happen to be King Arthur, change a commoner into a knight by saying "I dub thee Sir Knight." You can change your marital status by saying "I do thee wed" or, if you are fortunate enough to be a Muslim, "I do thee divorce." You can sign a paper making you a soldier for four years or a mortgage form making you a debtor for thirty years. In all these cases the change in status is accompanied by a corresponding change in social obligations. And, of course, by filling in the blank check of "I promise" you can take on new obligations without specifiable change in social status.

In all these cases it is the social or, as they are sometimes called, institutional facts that are changed, not the physical facts. The existence of social facts and, therefore, the possibility of changing them, is a consequence of the fact that agents are also persons living with others in social groups.

One could have the social institutions that create the possibility of social facts without the refinement that they could be changed merely by using words. You might, for example, achieve married status by cohabiting with someone for six months; become a debtor by accepting goods, services, or shelter; become a soldier by fighting in a war; and occupy a position of dignity and respect in the community by general consent. The possibility of doing something with words is created by an extension of the social institution which first made it possible to do what you do in any way at all.

I am inclined to think that things like warnings and frightenings operate through belief, changing the way someone who is told "There is a bull in the field," or "There is a horrible hairy spider crawling up your leg," sees his situation. Such statements are, therefore, more like constatives than performatives. However, the questions involved are complex. Provided some actions can be performed by means of words rather than by bodily movement, there cannot be a necessary connection between action and bodily movement. I hope I have said enough to establish this conclusion.

CHAPTER V

Beliefs and Intentions

1. Preliminary Remarks about Belief

In the previous chapter I pointed out that agents are persons, and that persons are also observers. In making observations people acquire beliefs. In this chapter I will consider the relationship between belief and action.

The account given of the relationship between belief and action will depend, in part, on the account given of belief. The concept of belief, however, is itself difficult to analyze. There are a number of different accounts of belief, reflecting and exemplifying fundamentally different views about the concept of mind and the relationship between the mental and the physical. In the next section I will try to sketch, very briefly, the main alternatives.

First a broad distinction must be made between two senses of belief. H. H. Price distinguishes between "belief that . . ." and "belief in."[1] To believe that . . . is to believe that something is the case; the belief therefore may be ex-

[1] Price, *Belief.*

pressed or described by means of a proposition, as in "John believes that there are mice in the wainscotting." This sort of belief might also be called propositional, since what is believed could be expressed or described by means of a proposition, even if it isn't. To believe in . . . is to believe in some person or thing, as in "John believes in God" or "Jill believes in North Sea Gas." This sort of belief might also be called nonpropositional. Since it is only propositions that can be verified as true or false, R. B. Braithwaite refers to the first sort of belief as verifiable belief, and to the second as unverifiable belief.[2] Clearly neither God nor North Sea Gas are the sort of thing that can be either true or false. And even if belief-in can be rephrased grammatically as belief-that—so that "John believes in God" becomes "John believes that God exists," and "Jill believes in North Sea Gas" becomes "Jill believes that North Sea Gas will provide cheap, efficient power"—the distinction between verifiable and unverifiable belief remains. Jill's belief is verifiable, but John's is not; for religious, ethical, and metaphysical statements are just those that fail to pass the verification test of cognitive meaning. Beliefs-in honesty, Marxism, and God do not become propositional, however expressed, since the propositions that purport to express them lack a method of verification and are not really propositions at all. Indeed, beliefs-in may have more in common with attitudes than with beliefs-that. It is obvious in any case that if the distinction between them is maintained, the relationship between belief-in and action may be different from that between belief-that and action. Here I will consider only the latter and henceforth use the word "belief" without qualification to mean "belief-that."

A second preliminary point is that, just as actions must be performed by somebody, so too beliefs must be held by somebody. In this sense beliefs have a psychological aspect

---

[2] Braithwaite, "Belief and Action" in *Supplement, Proceedings of the Aristotelian Society,* XVIII, 1946, pp. 2–5.

in addition to the epistemological aspect that they have in being propositional. What we say, in saying that John's belief that there are mice in the wainscotting is true or false or is or is not supported by evidence, has very little to do with the fact that it is *John's* belief that we are talking about, since we could say the same things about Jill's belief that there are mice in the wainscotting. The concept of belief is therefore both epistemological and psychological; and any account of it must reflect both these aspects and indicate the way they are related to each other.

2. Rival Accounts of Belief

I will refer to the two main accounts of belief as the occurrence account and the dispositional account. Dispositional properties may be attributed to both people and things, as, for example, in "Jill is afraid of mice" and "sugar is soluble." To say Jill is afraid of mice is to say that whenever Jill finds herself in the presence of a mouse she is terrified by it. Corresponding to Jill's fear of mice there are, or are likely to be, occasions on which Jill *is* afraid of a mouse. Such occasions are dateable events or occurrences, and provide the primary grounds for attributing the relevant disposition. To attribute a dispositional property is not itself to refer to any such dateable occurrence, but to say that such occurrences are likely to occur in certain circumstances. With respect to any dispositional property, therefore, it will always make sense to ask two questions: 1. *In which circumstances* will it display itself? (Thus Jill's fear of mice will display itself when Jill finds herself in the company of mice.) 2. *In what ways* will it display itself? (Thus Jill's fear of mice will display itself by Jill's shrieking, standing on a chair, giving a psychogalvanic skin response, and secreting adrenalin into her bloodstream.) In this example, the circumstances and the ways in which the disposition displays itself are apparent from the way in which the disposition is described. This will not be so obvious in all cases; from the fact that someone is described as neurotic we do not know the form that his neurotic behavior will take or the occasions on which it will display itself.

It would not be at all plausible to deny that there is *a* dispositional use of the word "belief"; to do so would mean that John no longer believes that there are mice in the wainscotting when he goes to bed or thinks of something else. The occurrence and the dispositional accounts agree therefore that "belief" has a dispositional use. But they differ in the account they give of the occurrences in which that disposition is displayed. According to the version of the occurrence account that I will consider, a disposition to believe is displayed in occurrences that are themselves beliefs; dispositions to believe are regarded as dependent on the occurrences of actual beliefs. If there are occurrences that are beliefs, what occurs might be either a mental act or event such as a judgment, thought, or idea; or a physical act or event such as behavior or bodily movement. In traditional versions of the occurrence account, such as that given by Hume and more recently by Price,[3] what occurs is said to be mental; though a physicalist version, according to which what occurs is physical—e.g., a particular brain process— would be possible. I will try to outline, very briefly, what I take to be the main features of the occurrence account, according to which what occurs is something mental.

According to Price's analysis in "Some Considerations about Belief" there are two elements in belief: 1. "the *entertaining* of a proposition" and 2. "the *assenting* to or *adopting* of that proposition."[4] Central to this account is the difficult notion of entertaining a proposition. "Entertaining a

[3] Price, "Some Considerations about Belief" in *Proceedings of the Aristotelian Society,* XXXV, 1934-35.

[4] *Ibid.,* p. 232.

proposition *p* is knowing what it would be like for an indicative sentence *s* to be true, or for some non-verbal symbol equivalent to it to be true."[5] To entertain a proposition it is necessary to understand that proposition or some symbolic equivalent. In addition, the person must be aware of the proposition, or have the proposition in mind, on a particular occasion. And nothing can be said about "what kind of awareness or 'having in mind'" is involved.[6] The entertaining of propositions "is the basic intellectual phenomenon" that "admits of no explanation or analysis," and in terms of which "all other forms of thinking have to be explained."[7]

In the second element in belief—assenting to a proposition—there are according to Price again two elements, a volitional one and an emotional one. "We begin . . . by entertaining *several* propositions (at least two) which are mutually exclusive. Let us suppose that we have lost the cat. We entertain the proposition that the cat is in the cupboard, that it is in the coal-scuttle, that it is behind the sofa. We consider or wonder about these three propositions, and as yet we believe none of them. But presently we hear a noise from the direction of the cupboard, and forthwith we assent to or *adopt* the proposition that the cat is in the cupboard."[8] The emotional element is the degree of confidence with which the belief is held.

I will now turn to the dispositional account of belief. A disposition must be displayed in some way; but a belief disposition need not be displayed in occurrences that are themselves beliefs. According to Ryle there are "higher grade dispositions . . . the exercises of which are indefinitely heterogeneous";[9] and belief is such a disposition. A belief therefore is displayed in a variety of occurrences, primarily

---

[5] Price, *Belief*, p. 193.
[6] *Ibid.*, p. 199.
[7] *Ibid.*, p. 192.
[8] Price, "Some Considerations about Belief," pp. 233–34.
[9] Ryle, *The Concept of Mind*, p. 44.

things said and done, none of which are themselves beliefs. According to Braithwaite's account in "The Nature of Believing," "I believe that p" means "the conjunction of two propositions: 1. I entertain p . . . and 2. I have a disposition to act as if p were true."[10] The first proposition reports the occurrence of an event, the entertaining of a proposition; the second attributes a disposition to act to the person having the belief. In a later article, however, Braithwaite is inclined to favor a dispositional account of entertaining a proposition. "If," he says, "the proposition entertained is expressed in a sentence, entertaining the proposition seems to me to be indistinguishable from understanding the sentence"; and understanding a sentence is to be explained "in terms of the understander's mental and physical reactions over a comparatively long period."[11]

If this move is made there are no occurrences that are themselves beliefs, and Braithwaite's account also becomes wholly dispositional. I will concentrate here on the second element in belief, having a disposition to act as if p were true, which is offered not only as "a criterion of genuine belief," but as "part of the actual meaning of believing."[12] One problem that arises in this account is saying what it is to act as if p were true, since the account would be circular if this were interpreted as "acting as if I believed that p was true." Braithwaite avoids circularity by offering an account of the action appropriate to the truth of p that makes no reference to my belief that p was true. To use Braithwaite's own example, my belief that strawberries are, to me, indigestible, consists of my entertaining the proposition "strawberries are indigestible" and of my being disposed to act as if that proposition were true. The *circumstances* in which this disposition displays itself are twofold: external circumstances, e.g., my being offered strawberries; and in-

[10] Braithwaite, "The Nature of Believing," *Proceedings of the Aristotelian Society*, XXXIII, 1932–33, p. 132.

[11] ———, "Belief and Action," p. 7.

[12] ———, "The Nature of Believing," p. 133.

ternal circumstances, e.g., my needs (or "instinctive tend-encies"), being of a certain sort such as "to preserve my health" or "to have indigestion (e.g., in order to avoid some unpleasant duty)."[13] In "Belief and Action" the internal circumstances are referred to as "springs of action" and in-clude "all those internal factors . . . which are causes, or part causes, of a man's goal-directed activity," that is, "the intentions, desires, wants, motives, instinctive needs, drives, of the believer at the time when an external occasion for the appropriate action arises."[14] The *way* in which the disposition displays itself is by the occurrence of the ap-propriate action, i.e., the action appropriate to the truth of "strawberries are, to me, indigestible." For example, the disposition is displayed by my accepting or rejecting the strawberries. "The appropriateness of my action consists in its satisfying my needs, and the satisfaction of my needs is something into which no element of belief, or indeed of any mental element, need enter."[15]

3. *Some Criticism of the Dispositional Account of Belief*

On the dispositional account of belief, a belief is a disposi-tion to act; the relationship between belief and action is therefore that of a disposition to the occurrences in which it is displayed. The account of belief, therefore, needs to be supplemented by an account of what occurs in the appro-priate circumstances, that is, by an account of action. Braith-waite gives no explicit account of action but appears to think of actions as a species of bodily movements, i.e., those

[13] *Ibid.*, p. 134.
[14] Braithwaite, "Belief and Action," p. 9.
[15] _____, "The Nature of Believing," p. 134.

that are caused by and tend to fulfill the agent's "springs of action," which are also thought of as physical. Ryle's account of intelligent performance, also, suggests that actions are a species of bodily movements, i.e., those that occur as exercises of a capacity disposition to make certain movements rather than others, the relevant movements being those that display know-how or skill by satisfying or tending to satisfy standards or criteria. Dispositions that are capacities are distinguished from those that are tendencies;[16] and beliefs are tendency dispositions displayed, *inter alia*, in actions. But the circumstances in which such tendencies are displayed are not made clear.

I have already discussed and rejected the view that actions are a species of bodily movements; here I will consider only the relationship which, in the dispositional account, exists between belief and action. The primary evidence for attributing any disposition is the occurrence of those events in which the disposition displays itself; in the case of a belief disposition, it is the occurrence of the relevant actions. The dispositional account therefore seems to leave no room for the possibility of attributing a belief to someone even though they had never acted upon that belief, either because circumstances in which it would be appropriate to do so had not arisen or, worse still, because even in the relevant circumstances the person failed to act on his belief. For example, a doctor may believe that smoking causes lung cancer but nevertheless smokes heavily. No doubt this example could be accommodated by insisting that the doctor does not really believe what he says he does; or by arguing that his needs include not only the avoidance of painful death in the future but also the pursuit of present pleasure. But the obvious thing to say is simply that people do not always act on their beliefs, even when they have every reason to do so; people are not always rational. Conversely, we sometimes act as if a proposition were true even

[16] Ryle, *The Concept of Mind*, p. 133.

though we do not believe it to be true. Price points out that "when we come to a fork in a road, and have no evidence as to which of the two branch-roads is the right one . . . , assent, and therefore belief, is impossible. We can only decide to act as if road A was the right one. But we do not on that account believe it."[17]

Counter examples, however, are not conclusive; there is a more fundamental objection to the dispositional account of belief. What is being offered is an account of belief that something is the case, e.g., that there are cookies in the cupboard; but the proposition whereby the belief in question is described is given a purely epistemological status. It is something that can be true or false, but not something that has any relation to the person holding the belief. If I believe that there are cookies in the cupboard I am disposed to act as if the proposition "There are cookies in the cupboard" were true. This disposition will display itself when I am hungry and when I am in the vicinity of the cupboard; in these circumstances I will go to the cupboard and, if there are any cookies there, eat them. But on a purely dispositional account of belief there is, and can be, no cause or reason for my going to the cupboard. There is no way in which the internal causes—in this case my hunger—can achieve external direction or orientation. The account, in according only an epistemological status to the proposition believed, ignores the fact that beliefs are held by people. And it is only because beliefs are held by people that they are available to people in guiding their actions. It is true that the disposition to act as if p were true is a disposition of the person holding the belief; but the believer is cut off from the cognitive content of his belief. There is no reason why I should go to the cupboard, however hungry; there is nothing to orient my movements in the direction of the cupboard. A proposition that is merely entertained, whether entertaining is a mental event or the capacity to

17 Price, "Some Considerations about Belief," p. 236.

understand a proposition, cannot fulfill this role. My behavior in going to the cupboard, if I do go, is wholly
mysterious and inexplicable. No account in terms of the
physical features of the situation will do; I cannot see the
cookies in the cupboard if the door is shut or if I am in the
garden. In any case I cannot see them if my belief is false
and there are no cookies in the cupboard to be seen. The
cupboard, of course, is there; and it might be argued that
I have learned to associate the cupboard with cookies, having found cookies there in the past. But I may have had no
previous acquaintance with the cupboard; beliefs may be
acquired verbally. The soldier in the story of the tinder box
knew that the dog with eyes as big as saucers was sitting
on a chest containing pennies, even though he had never
seen it before, because the old woman had told him so.

If then "acting as if p were true" is taken as "acting as if
p were believed to be true" the dispositional account is
circular; if it is not, the account is incoherent. In the next
section I will offer an account of the relationship between
belief and action according to which beliefs function as
guides to action. The discussion of belief in the preceding
sections has, I hope, prepared the ground for this, particularly by rejecting the suggestion that beliefs can be reduced
to actions or tendencies to act.

4. Belief and Action

In the previous section I argued that beliefs cannot be
reduced to actions or tendencies to act, and suggested that
beliefs function as guides to action. I will now try to ex-
pand on this.

Starting first from the side of belief, it will always make
sense to ask what action was based on any particular belief;
and a positive answer will often be available. Given my be-

lief that there are cookies in the cupboard, for example, I may go to the cupboard when I wake up hungry in the night. But for many beliefs a positive answer will not be available. There may be circumstances in which my belief that Caesar crossed the Rubicon or that my daughter has blue eyes would guide my actions, perhaps if I were planning an archaeological expedition or choosing a birthday gift. But even if no such circumstances ever occurred my beliefs would remain intelligible as beliefs.

Starting now from the side of action, it will again always make sense to ask, of any purported action, on what belief it was based. Brutus' action in stabbing Caesar, for example, was based on the belief that a particular individual, perhaps the one wearing the purple, was Caesar. No doubt it was based on other beliefs too, for example, on the belief that no member of his guard was close enough to protect Caesar; it would be arbitrary, and pointless, to try to list them all. Nor do the beliefs that guide an action necessarily remain the same during the course of the action; perhaps the second stab wound was inflicted only because it was believed that the first one failed to kill. But if it is claimed that Brutus was guided neither by these nor any other beliefs, then it does not make sense to say that the purported action was an action at all. Even if identical movements of Brutus' body occurred with the same fatal consequences, they would remain "mindless" movements if not guided by beliefs. It is of course highly unlikely that such identical movements would occur; a claim by Brutus that his mind "just went blank" would be received with skepticism. Thus Ryle's claim that intelligent performance need not be preceded by theorizing is incorrect if theorizing includes the acquisition of beliefs.

The dependence of action on belief is obscured in most cases by the fact that the relevant beliefs are so obvious that they are taken for granted. Of course Brutus believed that it was Caesar that he was stabbing; our interest is concentrated on other aspects of his action, particularly the part that it played in his political ambitions. In some cases, however, we may fail to understand an action because we are not aware of the beliefs on which it was based. One way of explaining an action, or making it intelligible, therefore, is by making explicit the beliefs on which it is based. For example, the boy is following the refuse cart because he thinks it is a wedding; the man is putting vinegar on his hair because he thinks it is hair lotion, or watering the bramble because he thinks it is a rosebush. In these cases the beliefs are not only false but also naïve, and they are unlikely to be shared by others; it is necessary to make them explicit in order to make the actions based on them intelligible. If a man waters a rosebush believing that it is a rosebush his action is dependent on his belief in the same way as when he waters the bramble because he believes it is a rosebush; but there is then no need to make that dependence explicit, and therefore it can easily pass unnoticed.

The beliefs on which an action is based may be false, as in the examples in the previous paragraph. If so the action will to some extent be "unhappy," to borrow Austin's phrase; but it will be an action nonetheless. But it is not possible for a person to act on beliefs that they regard as false; to say I regard a belief as false is to say that it is a belief that I do not hold. An action and the beliefs on which it is based are united in being beliefs and actions of the same person. Cases in which people pretend to act on beliefs that they know are false, or obey orders based on beliefs that they do not themselves share, present complications for this view but can be dealt with. For example, if I act as if I believed I were the inspector general when I know very well I am not, I am nevertheless acting on beliefs that I really hold, such as the belief that others do not know what the inspector general looks like, that they will treat the person they take to be the inspector general with respect, and so on.

The connection between belief and action is a conceptual one; one cannot say what an action is without saying that actions presuppose beliefs. But the connection between a particular action and the beliefs that it presupposes is contingent. My action in drinking from a glass on a given occasion may be based on the belief that the glass contains beer. But that I drink beer, when the opportunity offers, is a contingent fact about me. I may drink it; but I may also wash my hair in it, pour it down the sink, or make it the subject of a temperance lecture. I may say, or do, any of an almost infinite variety of things. It is this variety that makes the disposition to act as if, in the dispositional account of belief, so open-ended. Of course beer is brewed in order to be drunk, and that is probably what will happen to it. But if two people are both faced with a glass of beer and one drinks it and the other doesn't, this is unlikely to have anything to do with their beliefs. It is more likely to show that one of them likes beer and the other doesn't. We would normally base our opinion of their beliefs on the fact that both were in a position to see that there was a glass of beer on the table, and our opinion of their liking for beer on whether they drank the beer. In general our beliefs about the world depend on the way the world is; how we act in the light of those beliefs depends on the way we are.

Finally, action not only starts with belief; it also ends with it. Suppose that the cat that was on the mat is now in the garden, and that it is there as a result of my action. Then in doing what I did I changed things in such a way that the belief I had, that the cat is on the mat, is no longer appropriate. Moreover, since it is no longer appropriate as a result of something I did, I am well placed to know that this is so. One consequence of my action, therefore, is that whereas before I acted I believed that *p*, having acted I now believe that *not-p*. People do often act without paying attention to what they are doing, or forget what they have done right after they have done it. But these cases are the exceptions rather than the rule; they do not undermine the epistemological importance of action as a source of belief. It is equally true that we often see things without really looking at them, or forget soon afterward what we have seen; but these facts do not undermine the importance of the evidence of the senses as the basis of empirical knowledge. And the beliefs acquired as a result of acting will of course extend beyond those that consist only of the negation of the beliefs on which the action was based. Having put the cat in the garden I will not only cease to believe that it is on the mat, but will now believe that it is in the garden.

Other belief elements in action, which can only be mentioned here, are the agent's belief that such and such is the way to achieve his ends, and his belief that he can do such and such.

5. Intentionality

I have argued that the beliefs on which a person acts are an important part of his action, which is not intelligible as an action apart from those beliefs. But actions contain other elements as well. In the next section I will consider one of them, the intention with which a person acts. But first I will try to remove a possible source of confusion.

In previous chapters I have used the words "intention" and "intentional" on several occasions. In Chapter III, before discussing the view that consciousness is a brain process, I pointed out that when I perform an action I am aware of, or conscious of, what I am doing, and I said that when Brutus stabbed Caesar he knew what he was doing and intended to do it. Later I discussed the rule-following purposive model of action according to which actions are performed in order to bring about ends and, in considering the possibility of a physicalist account of intention, examined Smart's claim that "what is important in intention is not consciousness but goal-directedness."[18]

[18] See Chapter III, footnote 9.

At least two ideas are involved here. Instead of saying that when Brutus stabbed Caesar he knew what he was doing and intended to do it I might have said that Brutus stabbed Caesar intentionally. The force of the word "intentionally" here is to deny that what occurred was an accident or a natural event; or, putting it positively, to insist that stabbing Caesar was something Brutus *did*. It is *not* simply to say that Brutus stabbed Caesar with the intention of achieving some end, such as his death. It is obvious therefore that the notion of intentionality is complex and difficult to analyze, and I will not try to do so here. I will mention only Brentano's attempt to distinguish between mental and physical phenomena in terms of the intentionality or "intentional inexistence" that is the exclusive characteristic of the former. "Every mental phenomena," he said, "is characterised by . . . the intentional inexistence of an object, . . . the reference to a content, a direction upon an object (by which we are not to understand a reality in this case), or an immanent objectivity."[19] The main points are that all mental experience is directed toward an object, for example one who loves, loves something or someone; and that the object of the experience need have no existence independent of the experience. An example may make this clearer. In Hardy's novel, *Tess of the d'Urbervilles*, Tess confesses to Angel Clare that, prior to their marriage, she had been seduced by Alex d'Urberville. She asks him to forgive her but it is clear that he cannot do so, and the following conversation takes place.

"*'I thought, Angel, that you loved me—me, my very self! If it is I you do love, O how can it be that you look and speak so? It frightens me! Having begun to love you, I love you for ever—in all changes, in all disgraces, because you are yourself. I ask no more. Then how can you, O my own husband, stop loving me?'*

19 Brentano, "The Distinction Between Mental and Physical Phenomena," p. 50.

'I repeat, the woman I have been loving is not you.'
'But who?'
'Another woman in your shape.' "[20]

Thus Tess loved Angel Clare, who did exist, while Angel Clare loved "another woman" who existed only as the object of his love.

Brutus' action in stabbing Caesar does not seem to qualify as intentional as explained above. It was directed toward an object, Caesar, and Brutus was conscious of that object; but it could not have been directed toward that object if the object had not existed. In one sense this is true; but it is not true in the relevant sense. To adopt a favorite example of Russell's, Othello believed that Desdemona loved Cassio and, eventually, killed Cassio's lover; but Cassio had no lover, for Desdemona did not in fact love Cassio. Thus Othello killed Cassio's lover, though Cassio's lover possessed only intentional inexistence.

The second idea is the idea that actions are performed in order to, or with the intention of, bringing about ends. The intention with which a person acts is a principal element, together with belief, in action. In the next section I will try to summarize the picture of action that has emerged in this book, at the same time locating the place of intentions in that picture.

6. Intentions

To act is to act on something and so to change it. The something that is acted on and that becomes changed by the action is a state of affairs in the world. In human action the change is brought about by the agency of a person who is also an observer. The agent therefore has beliefs about the

[20] Hardy, *Tess of the d'Urbervilles*, p. 260.

situation in which and on which he is acting. He also has intentions about the way in which that situation is to be changed by his action.

In any case of action, therefore, the agent must see the situation that is to be changed by his action in some way; that is, he must hold some beliefs about it. For example, Brutus believed that Caesar was standing close by, alive, and free from stab wounds. The agent must also see the situation as subject to change that he is able to specify; Brutus realized that though Caesar was alive, he might be dead. The requirements that the situation be seen in some way and that it be seen as subject to change are not wholly independent. Beliefs-that are propositional in that what is believed could be expressed by a proposition even if it is not. Thus a language user who believed that Caesar is alive would accept the proposition "Caesar is alive" as true. But though true, it is not necessarily true. To acquire such a belief therefore is to receive information; it is to learn that of two states of affairs, both of which are possible, only one is in fact the case. The capacity exercised in believing that p might also have been exercised in believing that *not-p* or indeed that q is the case where q is inconsistent with p. To talk of entertaining and assenting to a proposition is to put this logical point in a psychological way.

Brutus did not merely realize, in an intellectual, detached sort of way, that though alive, Caesar might be dead. As a person he had the concept of himself as a person and therefore as an agent; and he saw the situation as alterable through his agency, i.e., as one that he could, or was able to, alter. He believed that if he stabbed Caesar, Caesar would die. He therefore stabbed Caesar with the intention of bringing about Caesar's death. His intention was to change the state of affairs obtaining in the world from that truly described by the proposition "Caesar is alive" to that truly described by "Caesar is dead." Thus intentions, like beliefs, are propositional; and actions successfully carried out are a source of belief.

Finally, Brutus wanted Caesar dead. He saw the state of affairs described by the proposition "Caesar is dead" as preferable to that described by "Caesar is alive." Thus beliefs, intentions, and wants are different modes of entertaining propositions or, to express it in another way, involve the possession and use, in different ways, of the conceptual scheme in terms of which the concept of a person was defined.

7. Conclusion

The plan of this book has been basically simple, perhaps naïvely so. Both actions and events that are not actions involve change. In the case of natural events, however, we attribute responsibility for the change to the occurrence of a prior event or events; in the case of actions we attribute responsibility for the change to a person. Consequently, the view taken about what an action is will depend on the view taken of what a person is. I therefore examined one view of action, that of Prichard, which is suggested by a basically Cartesian view of a person. I then considered a view of action that results if a Hobbesian view of a person is adopted; in this connection I examined the views of Smart and Ryle. In the course of considering criticism of these views I mentioned Peters' rule-following purposive model of action and Hart's ascriptivism, both of which stress the importance of the social context in which actions are performed. Neither the Cartesian nor the Hobbesian view, however, take the concept of agency sufficiently seriously. I was therefore led to look more closely at the concept of a person, relying on Strawson's account in *Individuals*, according to which the concept of a person cannot be dispensed with in favor of either that of a Cartesian ego or that of a human body. Agents, I suggested, are persons, and persons are observers as well as agents, and acquire beliefs through the observations they make. In this chapter therefore I discussed the relationship between belief and action.

The subject of action is an extremely large one, and many topics have necessarily been omitted. The nature of action has been discussed extensively in articles and books in connection with the so-called problem of free will and in connection with the problem of explanation in social science; the discussion is thereby broadened to include topics such as causality and the nature of explanation, which I have avoided. I have made no attempt to consider the detailed logic of words like "predicting," "deciding," "trying," "can," "wanting," "wishing," and "desiring." I have not considered the various sorts of adverbial qualifications that may be included in descriptions of actions, such as "freely," "deliberately," "voluntarily," "inadvertently," and so on. I have said little about our knowledge of actions, either our own or those of others; or about the social context in which actions are performed. I hope, however, that what has been included will serve as an introduction to the more detailed consideration of the many other topics within the philosophy of action and toward which it leads.

FURTHER READING[*]

---

[*] The numbers refer to entries in the bibliography.

CHAPTER III.   *Actions and Bodily Movements*

1. *Actions as a Subclass of Bodily Movements*
    Hobbes (23), Introduction, Chapters 1 and 6.
    Peters and Tajfel (326).
    For the elementary facts of the physiology of the hu-
        man body consult any textbook of physiological
        psychology, e.g., *Physiological Psychology* by M. A.
        Wenger, F. N. Jones, and M. H. Jones. Constable
        & Co., London, 1956. The facts regarding brain
        function are not so clear; see, e.g., J. Z. Young
        (52).

2. *Behaviorism in Psychology*
    Woodworth (50), Chapters 1, 3, and 4.
    Skinner, B. F. (365).

3. *Physicalism*
    Smart (40), Chapter 1.
    Hamlyn (217).

4. *The Identity Theory*
    Place (328).
    Smart (367).
    Smart (40), Chapters 4 and 5.
    Cf. also later in the present volume, Chapter 4, Sec-
        tion 2; and Chapter 5, Section 5 and references.
    Presley (67).

5. *Ryle's Account of Intelligent Performance*
    Smart (40), Chapter 6.
    Ryle (38), Chapters 1 and 2.

6. *Dispositions and Physicalism*
    Ryle (38), Chapter 5.
    Cf. later in the present volume, Chapter 5, Section 2.

7. *The Rule-following Purposive Model*
    Peters (33), Chapters 1 and 6.
    Melden (292).

On the social context of actions, see Winch (47), Chapters 2 and 5.
Taylor, Charles (42), Chapters 1 and 2.

8. *Ascriptivism*
    Hart (221).
    Hart (21).
    Taylor, Richard (43), Chapter 8.
    Geach (196).
    Pitcher (327).
    Austin, J. L. (7), Chapter 6, "A Plea for Excuses."
    Austin, J. L. (94).
    Feinberg (184).

9. *The Possibility of a Physicalist Account of Intentions*
    Smart (368).
    Taylor, Richard (43).

CHAPTER IV. *Persons and Agents*

1. *Actions and Those who Perform Them*
    Taylor, Richard (43), Chapter 9.

2. *Persons*
    Strawson (41), Part I. (The chapter on "Persons" cannot be fully understood independently of the earlier chapters.)

3. *Observers and Agents*
    Hampshire (17), Chapter 1.
    Wittgenstein (49), Part I, Sections 1–17.
    On action and bodily movement see Hamlyn (216) and Melden (30), Chapter 6.
    Acts of omission are discussed in D'Arcy (13), Chapter 1, Section 2.

4. *Doing Things with Words*
    Austin, J. L. (7), foot of pp. 65–71.

Austin, J. L. (93)—a short statement of the position
  elaborated in (7).
On institutional facts see Anscombe (80).

CHAPTER V.   *Beliefs and Intentions*

1. *Preliminary Remarks about Belief*
   Price (35), p. 76 and Series II, Lecture 9.
   Braithwaite (118).

2. *Rival Accounts of Belief*
   Price (331) and (35).
   Braithwaite (117).
   Ryle (38), pp. 28, 44, 118, and 133–35.

3. *Some Criticism of the Dispositional Account of Be-
   lief*
   Price (35).
   O'Connor, D. J. (309).

4. *Belief and Action*
   For clarification of what is meant by the phrase "conceptual connection" see Ryle (37), Chapter 8.

5. *Intentionality*
   Cornman (151).
   Chisholm (136).
   Chisholm (12), Chapter 11.
   Kenny (25), Chapter 9.
   Brown (131).

6. *Intentions*
   Cf. previously in present volume, Chapter 3, Section
   9 and references.
   Anscombe (79).
   Passmore (318).
   On wants see:
     Hare (220).
     Anscombe (1), Sections 36–40.

Melden (30), Chapters 10, 11, and 12.
Kenny (25), Chapter 5.
McGuiness (288).
Daveney (159).

BIBLIOGRAPHY

BOOKS

(1) Anscombe, G. E. M., *Intention*. Blackwell, 1957; Ithaca, New York: Cornell University Press, 1957.

(2) Armstrong, D. M., *A Materialist Theory of the Mind*. Routledge & Kegan Paul, 1968.

(3) Ashby, W. R., *Design for a Brain*. Chapman & Hall, 1954; New York: Barnes & Noble, 1966.

(4) Asimov, I., *The Human Brain, Its Capabilities and Functions*. Nelson, 1965; New American Library, New York.

(5) Aristotle, *The Ethics of Aristotle—The Nichomachean Ethics*. Translated by J. A. K. Thomason. Penguin Classics, 1953. (See esp. Book III, Chapters 1 to 5 and Book V, Chapter 8); Baltimore: Penguin Books, 1955.

(6) Austin, J., *Lectures on Jurisprudence*. Lectures XVIII to XXI. 5th edition by Robert Campbell. Murray, 1885; New York: Humanities Press, 1965.

(7) Austin, J. L., *Philosophical Papers*. Oxford, 1961.

(8) ———, *How to Do Things with Words*. Oxford, 1962; New York: Oxford University Press, 1965.

(9) Ayers, M. R., *The Refutation of Determinism: An Es-*

say in Philosophical Logic. Methuen, 1968; New
York, 1968.

(10) Bennett, J., *Rationality.* Routledge & Kegan Paul,
1964; New York: Humanities Press, 1964.

(11) Brown, D. G., *Action.* Allen & Unwin, 1968; Toronto: University of Toronto Press, 1968.

(12) Chisholm, R. M., *Perceiving.* Ithaca, New York: Cornell University Press, 1957 (see esp. Chap. 11).

(13) D'Arcy, E., *Human Acts: An Essay in Their Moral
Evaluation.* Oxford, 1963.

(14) Descartes, R., *Discourse on Method.* Everyman, 1912;
Dutton, New York.

(15) Dray, W., *Laws and Explanation in History.* Oxford,
1957 (see esp. Chap. 5).

(16) Gardiner, P., *The Nature of Historical Explanation,*
Part IV. Oxford, 1952.

(17) Hampshire, S., *Thought and Action.* Chatto & Windus, 1959; New York: Viking Press, 1960.

(18) ———, *The Freedom of the Individual.* Chatto &
Windus, 1965; New York: Harper & Row, 1965.

(19) Hardy, T., *Tess of the d'Urbervilles.* Papermac Edition. New York: St. Martin's Press, 1891.

(20) Hart, H. L. A., *Punishment and Responsibility.* Oxford, 1961.

(21) ———, *The Concept of Law.* Oxford, 1961.

(22) ———, and Honoré, M., *Causation in the Law.* Oxford, 1959.

(23) Hobbes, T., *Leviathan.* Edited by Michael Oakeshott.
Blackwell, Oxford; New York: Barnes & Noble,
1966.

(24) Hudson, D. W., *Modern Moral Philosophy.* Doubleday, 1970 (see Chap. 7).

(25) Kenny, A., *Action, Emotion and Will.* Routledge &
Kegan Paul, 1963; New York: Humanities Press,
1963.

(26) Kenny, C. S., *Outlines of Criminal Law.* 16th edition

by J. W. Cecil Turner. Cambridge, 1952; New York: Cambridge University Press, 1958.

(27) Louch, A. R., *Explanation and Human Action*. Blackwell, 1966; Berkeley: University of California Press, 1969.

(28) Macmurray, J., *The Self as Agent*. Faber & Faber, 1957; New York: Humanities Press, 1957.

(29) Meiland, J. W., *The Nature of Intention*. Methuen, 1970.

(30) Melden, A. I., *Free Action*. Routledge & Kegan Paul, 1961, New York: Humanities Press.

(31) Moore, G. E., *Ethics*. Hutchinsons University Library, 1912 (see Chap. 6). New York: Oxford University Press, 1912.

(32) Nowell-Smith, P. H., *Ethics, Part II, Choosing and Advising*. Baltimore: Penguin Books, 1954.

(33) Peters, R. S., *The Concept of Motivation*. Routledge & Kegan Paul, 1958; New York: Humanities Press, 1970.

(34) Powell, B., *Knowledge of Actions*. Allen & Unwin, 1966; New York: Humanities Press, 1967.

(35) Price, H. H., *Belief*. Allen & Unwin, 1969; New York: Humanities Press, 1970.

(36) Prichard, H. A., *Moral Obligation*. Oxford, 1949.

(37) Ryle, G., *Dilemmas*. Cambridge, 1954.

(38) ———, *The Concept of Mind*. Hutchinson, 1949; New York: Barnes & Noble, 1949.

(39) Shwayder, D. S., *The Stratification of Behaviour*. Routledge & Kegan Paul, 1965; New York: Humanities Press, 1963.

(40) Smart, J. J. C., *Philosophy and Scientific Realism*. Routledge & Kegan Paul, 1963; New York: Humanities Press, 1963.

(41) Strawson, P. F., *Individuals*. Methuen, 1959.

(42) Taylor, C., *The Explanation of Behaviour*. Routledge & Kegan Paul, 1964; New York: Humanities Press, 1964.

(43) Taylor, R., *Action and Purpose*. Englewood Cliffs, New Jersey: Prentice-Hall, 1966.

(44) Vesey, G. N. A., *The Embodied Mind*. Allen & Unwin, 1965 (see Chaps. 5 and 11). New York: Humanities Press, 1965.

(45) White, A., *The Philosophy of Mind*. New York: Random House, 1967 (see Chap. 6).

(46) Williams, G., *Criminal Law, The General Part*. Stevens, 1961 (see Chap. 1).

(47) Winch, P., *The Idea of a Social Science*. Routledge & Kegan Paul, 1958; New York: Humanities Press, 1970.

(48) Wittgenstein, L., *Tractatus Logico-Philosophicus*. Routledge & Kegan Paul, 1961; New York: Humanities Press.

(49) ——, *Philosophical Investigations*. Blackwell, 1953; New York: Barnes & Noble, 1969.

(50) Woodworth, R. S., *Contemporary Schools of Psychology*. Methuen, 1948 (see Chaps. 3 and 4); New York: Ronald Press Company, 1964.

(51) von Wright, G. H., *Norm and Action: A Logical Enquiry*. Routledge & Kegan Paul, 1963.

(52) Young, J. Z., *A Model of the Brain*. Oxford, 1964.

COLLECTIONS OF ARTICLES

(53) Anderson, A. R. (ed.), *Minds and Machines*. Englewood Cliffs, New Jersey: Prentice-Hall, 1964.

(54) Berofsky, B. (ed.), *Free Will and Determinism*. New York: Harper & Row, 1966.

(55) Brand, M. (ed.), *The Nature of Human Action*. Glenview, Illinois: Scott, Foresman and Company, 1970. (Selections are divided into three sections: Action and Behaviour; Ability and Possibility; and Action and Logical Systems. Each is preceded by

an introduction by the editor. Includes a full bibliography.)

(56) Braybrooke, D. (ed.), *Philosophical Problems of the Social Sciences*. New York: The Macmillan Company, 1965.

(57) Edwards, P. (ed.), *The Encyclopedia of Philosophy*. New York: The Free Press, 1967 (see individual articles, esp. "Choosing, Deciding and Doing"; "Intentionality").

(58) Hook, S. (ed.), *Dimensions of Mind*. Collier Books, 1961 (see esp. Part III, "Concept-Formation").

(59) Hook, S., *Determinism and Freedom*. Collier Books, 1961 (see esp. Part III, "Determinism and Responsibility in Law and Ethics").

(60) *Inquiry*, Nos. 1–2. Summer 1970, Vol. 13 (devoted to articles on action).

(61) Lehrer, K. (ed.), *Freedom and Determinism*. New York: Random House, 1966.

(62) *Monist*. Vol. 49, No. 2, April 1965 (devoted to Agent and Spectator).

(63) Morgenbesser, S. T., and Walsh, J. J. (eds.), *Free Will*. Englewood Cliffs, New Jersey: Prentice-Hall, 1962.

(64) Morris, D. F. (ed.), *Freedom and Responsibility*. Stanford, California: Stanford University Press, 1961.

(65) O'Connor, J., and Fogelin, R. J., *Modern Materialism: Readings on Body-Mind Identity*. New York: Harcourt, Brace & World, 1969.

(66) Pears, D. F. (ed.), *Freedom and the Will*. New York: The Macmillan Company, 1963.

(67) Presley, C. F. (ed.), *The Identity Theory of Mind*. St. Lucia: Queensland University Press, 1967.

(68) Rescher, N. (ed.), *The Logic of Decision and Action*. University of Pittsburgh Press, 1967.

(69) *Royal Institute of Philosophy Lectures*. Vol. 1,

1966–67. *The Human Agent.* New York: The
Macmillan Company, 1968.

(70) Strawson, P. F. (ed.), *Studies in the Philosophy of
Thought and Action.* (British Academy Lectures,
introduced by P. F. Strawson). Oxford, 1968.

(71) Wann, T. W., *Behaviorism and Phenomenology.*
Phoenix Books, University of Chicago Press, 1964.

(72) White, A. R. (ed.), *The Philosophy of Action.* Oxford, 1968. (Includes an introduction by the editor
and a bibliography arranged under the following
headings: The Nature of Action, Descriptions of
Action, and Explanations of Action.)

ARTICLES

Abbreviations for Journals

A	Analysis
AJP	Australasian Journal of Philosophy
APQ	American Philosophical Quarterly
BJPS	British Journal for the Philosophy of Science
JP	Journal of Philosophy
M	Mind
P	Philosophy
PAS	Proceedings of the Aristotelian Society
PPR	Philosophy and Phenomenological Research
PQ	Philosophical Quarterly
PR	Philosophical Review
Pr.B.A.	Proceedings of the British Academy
SPAS	Proceedings of the Aristotelian Society, Supple-mentary Volume.

(73) Abelson, R., "Because I want to." *M* LXXIV, 1965,
pp. 540–53.

(74) ——, "Persons, P-predicates, and Robots." *APQ* Vol.
3, 1966, pp. 306–11.

(75) ——, "Doing, Causing, and Causing to Do." *JP* LXVI, 1969, pp. 178–92.

(76) Albritton, R., "Mere Robots and Others." *JP* LXI, 1964, pp. 691–94.

(77) Aldrich, V. C., "Behavior, Simulating and Non-simulating." *JP* LXIII, 1966, pp. 453–57.

(78) ——, "On Seeing Bodily Movements as Actions." *APQ* Vol. 4, 1967, pp. 222–30.

(79) Anscombe, G. E. M., "Intention." *PAS* Vol. LVIII, 1956–57, pp. 321–32. Reprinted in White, A. R., (ed.) [(72) above] and in *Essays in Philosophical Psychology*, edited by Donald F. Gustafson, Garden City, New York: Doubleday & Company, 1964.

(80) ——, "On Brute Facts." *A* XVIII, 1958, pp. 69–72.

(81) ——, "On Sensations of Position." *A* XXII, 1961–62, pp. 55–58.

(82) ——, "Two Kinds of Error in Action." *JP* LX, 1963, pp. 393–401.

(83) Ardal, P. S., "Motives, Intentions and Responsibility." *PQ* Vol. 15, 1965, pp. 146–53.

(84) Armstrong, D. M., "Dispositions are Causes." *A* XXX, 1969–70, pp. 23–26.

(85) Ashby, W. R., "The Nervous System as a Physical Machine: With Special Reference to the Origin of Adaptive Behavior." *M* LVI, 1947, pp. 45–59.

(86) Aune, B., "Abilities, Modalities and Free-will." *PPR* XXIII, 1962–63, pp. 397–413.

(87) ——, "Intention and Foresight." *JP* LXIII, 1966, pp. 652–54.

(88) ——, "Hypotheticals and 'Can': Another Look." *A* XXVII, 1966–67, pp. 191–95.

(89) ——, "Free Will, 'Can' and Ethics: A Reply to Lehrer." *A* XXX, 1969–70, pp. 77–83.

(90) Austin, J. L., "Other Minds." *SPAS* XX, 1946. Reprinted in Austin, J. L. [(7) above]; also in *Logic and Language,* edited by A. G. N. Flew, Blackwell,

1953; in White, A. R., (ed.) [(72) above]; and in *Ordinary Language,* edited by V. C. Chappell, Englewood Cliffs, New Jersey: Prentice-Hall, 1964.

(91) ———, "Ifs and Cans." *Pr.B.A.* XLII, 1956, pp. 109–32. Reprinted in Austin, J. L. [(7) above].

(92) ———, "A Plea for Excuses." *PAS* LVIII, 1956–57, pp. 1–30. Also in Austin, J. L. [(7) above]. Reprinted in White, A. R., (ed.) [(72) above].

(93) ———, "Performative-Constative." *In Philosophy and Ordinary Language,* edited by C. E. Caton, translation by G. J. Warnock. University of Illinois Press, 1963.

(94) ———, "Three Ways of Spilling Ink." *PR* LXXV, 1966.

(95) Ayer, A. J., "Man as a Subject for Science." August Comte Memorial Lecture, L.S.E., 1964; printed in *Philosophy, Politics and Society,* third series, edited by Peter Laslett and W. G. Runciman, Blackwell, 1967. Also in Ayer's *Metaphysics and Commonsense,* New York: The Macmillan Company, 1969.

(96) Ayers, M. R., "Austin on 'Could' and 'Could Have.'" *PQ* Vol. 16, 1966, pp. 113–20.

(97) ———, "Perception and Action" in *Knowledge and Necessity, Royal Institute of Philosophy Lectures, Vol.* 3, 1968–69. New York: The Macmillan Company, 1970.

(98) Baier, K., "Decisions and Descriptions." *M* LX, 1951, pp. 181–204.

(99) ———, "Could and Would." *A* XXII, 1962–63, pp. 20–29.

(100) ———, "Reasons for Doing Something." *JP* LXI, 1964, pp. 198–203.

(101) ———, "Action and Agent." *Monist* Vol. 49, 1965, pp. 183–95.

(102) ———, "Acting and Producing." *JP* LXII, 1965, pp. 645–48.

(103) ———, "Responsibility and Action." In Brand, M. (ed.) [(55) above].

(104) Barnes, W. H. F., "Action." *M* L, 1941, pp. 243–57.

(105) Beck, L. W., "Agent, Actor, Spectator, and Critic." *Monist* Vol. 49, 1965, pp. 167–82.

(106) ———, "Conscious and Unconscious Motives." *M* LXXV, 1966, pp. 155–79.

(107) Bedford, E., "Intention and Law." *JP* LXIII, 1966, pp. 654–56.

(108) Bell, D. R., "The Idea of a Social Science." *SPAS* XLI, 1967, pp. 115–32.

(109) Bennett, D., "Action, Reason and Purpose." *JP* LXII, 1965, pp. 85–96.

(110) ———, "Rationality of Jonathan Bennett." (Review) *JP* LXIII, 1966, pp. 262–66.

(111) Bennett, J., "Whatever the Consequences." *A* XXVI, 1965–66, pp. 83–102.

(112) ———, "Acting and Refraining." *A* XXVIII, 1967–68, pp. 30–31.

(113) Benson, J., "The Characterisation of Actions and the Virtuous Agent." *PAS* LXIII, 1962–63, pp. 251–66.

(114) Black, M., "Austin on Performatives." *P* XXXVIII, 1963, pp. 217–26.

(115) Blanshard, B. and Skinner, B. F., "The Problem of Consciousness—a Debate." *PPR* XXVII, 1966–67, pp. 317–37.

(116) Bradley, F. H., "The Vulgar Notion of Responsibility in Connection with the Theories of Freewill and Necessity." Essay I in Bradley's *Ethical Studies*. Oxford, 1961.

(117) Braithwaite, R. B., "The Nature of Believing." *PAS* XXXIII, 1932–33, pp. 129–46. Reprinted in *Knowledge and Belief*, edited by A. Phillips Griffiths, Oxford 1967.

(118) ———, "Belief and Action." *SPAS* XVIII, 1946, pp. 1–19.

(119) ———, "Teleological Explanation." *PAS* XLVII, 1946–47, pp. i–xx.

(120) ———, "An Empiricist's View of the Nature of Religious Belief." Eddington Memorial Lecture for 1955, Cambridge University Press. Reprinted in *Christian Ethics and Contemporary Philosophy*, edited by Ian T. Ramsey.

(121) ———, "Belief as Setting the Stage for Decision." In *Decision Making* edited by R. J. Audley, B.B.C. Publication, 1967, pp. 27–39.

(122) Brandt, R. and Kim, J., "Wants as Explanations of Actions." *JP* LX, 1963, pp. 425–35.

(123) Braybrooke, D. et al., "Some Questions for Miss Anscombe About Intention." *A* XXII, 1961–62, pp. 47–54.

(124) Brentano, F., "The Distinction Between Mental and Physical Phenomena." Translated by D. B. Terrell in *Realism and the Background of Phenomenology*, edited by R. M. Chisholm. Illinois Free Press, 1960, pp. 39–61.

(125) Broadie, F., "Trying and Doing." *PAS* LXVI, 1965–66, pp. 27–40.

(126) ———, "Knowing That I am Doing." *PQ* Vol. 17, 1967, pp. 137–49.

(127) Brodbeck, M., "Meaning and Action." *Philosophy of Science*, Vol. 30, 1963, pp. 309–24. (Reprinted in *The Philosophy of Science*, edited by P. H. Nidditch, Oxford 1968.)

(128) Bronaugh, R. N., "The Logic of Ability Judgments." *PQ* Vol. 18, 1968, pp. 122–30.

(129) Brown, R., "On Having One's Reasons." *P* XXXVIII, 1963, pp. 264–71.

(130) Brown, S. C., "Intentionality Intensified." *PQ* Vol. 13, 1963, pp. 357–60.

(131) ———, "Intentionality Without Grammar." *PAS* LXV, 1964–65, pp. 123–46.

(132) Canfield, J., "Knowing About Future Decisions." *A* XXII, 1961–62, pp. 127–29.

(133) Cargile, J., "Davidson's Notion of Logical Form." *Inquiry* Vol. 13, pp. 129–39.

(134) Castañeda, H. N., "The Logic of Change, Action, and Norms." *JP* LXII, 1965 (review article), pp. 333–44.

(135) Chappell, V. C., "Causation and the Identification of Actions." *JP* LX, 1963, pp. 700–1.

(136) Chisholm, R. M., "Sentences About Believing." *PAS* LVI, 1955–56, pp. 125–48.

(137) ———, "What Is It to Act upon a Proposition?" *A* XXII, 1961–62, pp. 1–6.

(138) ———, "The Descriptive Element in the Concept of Action." *JP* LXI, pp. 613–25.

(139) ———, "He Could Not Have Done Otherwise." *JP* LXIV, 1967, pp. 409–17.

(140) ———, "Freedom and Action." In Lehrer, K. (ed.) [(61) above], pp. 28–44. Reprinted in Brand, M. (ed.) [(55) above].

(141) Chopra, Y. N., "The Consequences of Human Actions." *PAS* LXV, 1964–65, pp. 147–66.

(142) Clark, M., "Intentional Objects." *A* XXV, 1964–65, pp. 121–28.

(143) Cody, A. B., "Can a Single Action Have Many Different Descriptions?" *Inquiry* Vol. 10, 1967, pp. 164–80.

(144) ———, "Reply to Mr. Dowling." *Inquiry* Vol. 10, 1967, pp. 449–52.

(145) Cohen, L. J., "Criteria of Intensionality." *SPAS* XLII, 1968, pp. 122–42.

(146) Cohen, M. D., "The Same Action." *PAS* LXX, 1969–70, pp. 75–90.

(147) Cohen, M. F., "Motives, Causal Necessity and Moral Accountability." *AJP* XLII, 1964, pp. 323–34.

(148) Cohen, S. M. and Mathews, G. B., "Wants and Lacks." *JP* LXIV, 1967, pp. 455–56.

(149) Coleman, D., "Cognition and the Will." *JP* LXI, 1964, pp. 155–58.

(150) Collins, A. W., "Jonathan Bennett on Rationality." (Review) *JP* LXIII, 1966, pp. 253–61.

(151) Cornman, J. W., "Intentionality and Intensionality." *PQ* Vol. 12, 1962, pp. 44–52.

(152) ———, "The Extent of Intentionality." *PQ* Vol. 14, 1964, pp. 355–57.

(153) Cowan, J. L., "Purpose and Teleology." *Monist* Vol. 52, 1968, pp. 317–28.

(154) ———, "Deliberation and Determinism." *APQ* Vol. 6, 1969, pp. 53–61.

(155) Danto, A. C., "What We Can Do." *JP* LX, 1963, pp. 435–45.

(156) ———, "Basic Actions." *APQ* Vol. 2, 1965, pp. 141–48. Reprinted in White, A. R. (ed.) [(72) above] and in Brand, M. (ed.) [(55) above].

(157) ———, "Causation and Basic Actions." *Inquiry* Vol. 13, 1970, pp. 108–25.

(158) Danto, A. C. and Morgenbesser, S., "Character and Free Will." *JP* LIV, 1957, pp. 493–505.

(159) Daveney, T. F., "Wanting." *PQ* Vol. 11, 1961, pp. 135–44.

(160) ———, "Choosing." *M* LXXIII, 1964, pp. 515–26. Reprinted in Brand, M. (ed.) [(55) above].

(161) ———, "Intentions and Causes." *A* XXVII, 1966–67, pp. 23–28.

(162) Davidson, D., "Actions, Reasons and Causes." *JP* LX, 1963, pp. 685–700. Reprinted in White, A. R. (ed.) [(72) above] and in Brand, M. (ed.) [(55) above].

(163) ———, "Action and Reaction." *Inquiry* Vol. 13, 1970, pp. 140–48.

(164) Deutch, K. W., "Mechanism, Teleology, and Mind." *PPR* XIII, 1951–52, pp. 185–223.

(165) Donnellan, K. S., "Knowing What I Am Doing." *JP* LX, 1963, pp. 401–9.

(166) Dore, C., "On the Meaning of 'Could Have.'" *A* XXII, 1962–63, pp. 41–42.

(167) ———, "More on the Meaning of 'Could Have.'" *A* XIV, 1963–64, pp. 41–43.

(168) ———, "On Being Able to Do Otherwise." *PQ* Vol. 16, 1966, pp. 137–45.

(169) Dowling, R. E., "Can an Action Have Many Descriptions?" *Inquiry* Vol. 10, 1967, pp. 447–48.

(170) Downie, R. S., "Roles and Moral Agency." *A* XXIX, 1968–69, pp. 39–42.

(171) Dray, W., "Choosing and Doing." *Dialogue* 1, 1962, pp. 129–52.

(172) ———, "The Historical Explanation of Actions Reconsidered." In *Philosophy and History*, edited by Sydney Hook. New York: New York University Press, 1963.

(173) Ducasse, C. J., "Life Telism and Mechanism." *PPR* XX, 1959–60, pp. 18–24.

(174) Duggan, T. and Gert, B., "Voluntary Abilities." *APQ* Vol. 4, 1967, pp. 127–35.

(175) Duncan-Jones, A., "Intention, Motive and Responsibility." *SPAS* XIX, 1945, pp. 267–88.

(176) ———, "Actions Speak Louder Than Words." *P* XXXV, 1960, pp. 306–13.

(177) ———, "Notional Choice." *PAS* LXI, 1960–61, pp. 1–18.

(178) Evans, J. L., "Knowledge and Behavior." *PAS* LIV, 1953–54, pp. 27–48.

(179) ———, "Choice." *PQ* Vol. 5, 1955, pp. 303–15.

(180) Ewin, R. E., "Actions, Brain-processes, and Determinism." *M* LXXVII, 1968, pp. 417–19.

(181) Ewing, A. C., "Mental Acts." *M* LVII, 1948, pp. 201–20.

(182) ———, "May Can-statements be Analyzed Deterministically?" *PAS* LXIV, 1963–64, pp. 157–76.

(183) Falk, W. D., "Action-guiding Reasons." *JP* LX, 1963, pp. 702–18.

(184) Feinberg, J., "Action and Responsibility." *In Philosophy in America,* edited by Max Black. Allen & Unwin, 1965. Reprinted in White, A. R. (ed.) [(72) above].

(185) Fingarette, H., "Performatives." *APQ* Vol. 4, 1967, pp. 39–48.

(186) Fitzgerald, P. J., "Voluntary and Involuntary Acts" in *Oxford Essays in Jurisprudence* edited by A. G. Guest. Clarendon Press, 1961. Reprinted in White, A. R. (ed.) [(72) above].

(187) ———, "Acting and Refraining." *A* XXVII, 1966–67, pp. 133–39.

(188) Fleming, B. N., "On Intention." *PR* LXXIII, 1964, pp. 301–20.

(189) Foot, P., "Free Will as Involving Determinism." *PR* LXVI, 1957, pp. 439–50. Reprinted in Morgenbesser, S. T. and Walsh, J. J. (eds.) [(63) above].

(190) Forguson, L. W., "In Pursuit of Performatives." *P* XLI, 1966, pp. 341–47.

(191) ———, "Austin's Philosophy of Action." *Archives de Philosophie,* 1967. Reprinted in translation in *Symposium on J. L. Austin,* edited by K. T. Fann. Routledge & Kegan Paul, 1969.

(192) Frankfurt, H. G., "Alternative Possibilities and Moral Responsibility." *JP* LXVI, 1969, pp. 829–39.

(193) Gallie, I., "Intelligence and Intelligent Conduct." *PAS* XLVIII, 1947–48, pp. 187–204.

(194) Gauthier, D. P., "How Decisions are Caused." *JP* LXIV, 1967, pp. 147–51.

(195) ———, "How Decisions are Caused (but not predicted)." *JP* LXV, 1968, pp. 170–71.

(196) Geach, P. T., "Ascriptivism." *PR* LXIX, 1960, pp. 221–25.

(197) George, R. A., "Acting Upon a Proposition." *A* XXII, 1962–63, pp. 116–18.

(198) Gibson, Q., "The Limits of Social Prediction." *Monist* Vol. 52, 1968, pp. 359–73.

(199) Ginet, C., "Can the Will be Caused?" *PR* LXXI, 1962, pp. 49–55.
(200) Glasgow, W. D., "On Choosing." *A* XVII, 1956–57, pp. 135–39.
(201) ———, "The Concept of Choosing." *A* XX, 1959–60, pp. 63–67.
(202) Goldberg, B., "Can a Desire be a Cause?" *A* XXV, 1964–65, pp. 70–72.
(203) Goldberg, B. and Heidelberger, H., "Mr. Lehrer on the Constitution of Cans." *A* XXI, 1960–61, p. 96. Reprinted in Brand, M. (ed.) [(55) above].
(204) Goldman, A. I., "Actions, Predictions and Books of Life." *APQ* Vol. 5, 1968, pp. 135–51.
(205) ———, "The Compatibility of Mechanism and Purpose." *PR* LXXVIII, 1969, pp. 468–82.
(206) Gordon, L. M., "The Range of Application of 'Voluntary,' 'Not Voluntary' and 'Involuntary.'" *A* XXVI, 1965–66, pp. 149–52.
(207) Grant, C. K., "Good At." *SPAS* XXXII, 1958, pp. 173–94.
(208) ———, "Belief and Action." Inaugural Lecture, University of Durham, 1960, Published by University of Durham.
(209) Griffin, J., "Consequences." *PAS* LXV, 1964–65, pp. 167–82.
(210) Griffiths, A. P., "Acting with Reason." *PQ* Vol. 8, 1958, pp. 289–99.
(211) Gunderson, K., "Interview with a Robot." *A* XXII, 1962–63, pp. 136–42.
(212) ———, "Robots, Consciousness, and Programmed Behavior." *BJPS* Vol. 19, 1968–69, pp. 109–22.
(213) Gustafson, D. F., "Voluntary and Involuntary." *PPR* XXIV, 1963–64, pp. 493–501.
(214) ———, "Monetary Intentions." *M* LXXVII, 1968, pp. 1–13.
(215) Haksar, V., "Responsibility." *SPAS* XL, 1966, pp. 187–222.

(216) Hamlyn, D. W., "Behavior." *P* XXVIII, 1953, pp. 132–45. Reprinted in *The Philosophy of Mind*, edited by V. C. Chappell. Englewood Cliffs, New Jersey: Prentice-Hall, 1962.

(217) ——, "Causality and Human Behavior." *SPAS* XXXVIII, 1964, pp. 125–42.

(218) Hampshire, S., "Walsh on *Thought and Action*." *JP* LX, 1963, pp. 410–24.

(219) Hannay, A. H., "Action." *PAS* XLII, 1941–42, pp. 141–50.

(220) Hare, R. M., "Descriptivism." *Pr.B.A.* XLIX, 1963, pp. 115–34.

(221) Hart, H. L. A., "The Ascription of Responsibility and Rights." *PAS* XLIX, 1948–49, pp. 171–94. Reprinted in *Logic and Language*, first series, edited by A. G. N. Flew. Blackwell, 1953.

(222) Hart, H. L. A. and Hampshire, S., "Decision, Intention and Certainty." *M* LXVII, 1958, pp. 1–12.

(223) Heath, P. L., "Intention." *SPAS* XXIX, 1955, pp. 147–64.

(224) Hedman, C. G., "On the Individuation of Actions." *Inquiry* Vol. 13, 1970, pp. 125–28.

(225) ——, "Intending the Impossible." *P* XLV, No. 71, 1970, pp. 33–38.

(226) Hempel, C. G., "Rational Action." *Proceedings and Addresses of the American Philosophical Association* XXXV, pp. 5–23. Yellow Springs, Ohio: The Antioch Press, 1962.

(227) Herbst, P., "Freedom and Prediction." *M* LXVI, 1957, pp. 1–27.

(228) Holdcroft, D., "A Plea for Excuses." *P* XLV, 1969, pp. 314–30.

(229) Hollis, M., "Conversation Piece." *A* XXII, 1962–63, pp. 142–44.

(230) Honoré, A. M., "Can and Can't." *M* LXXIII, 1964, pp. 463–79.

(231) Houlgate, L., "Acts Owing to Ignorance." *A* XXVII, 1966–67, pp. 17–22.

(232) Hunter, J. F. M., "Aune and Others on Ifs and Cans." *A* XVIII, 1967–68, pp. 107–9.

(233) Imlay, R. A., "Do I Ever Directly Raise My Arm?" *P* XLII, 1967, pp. 119–27.

(234) Jager, R., "Describing Acts Owing to Ignorance." *A* XXVII, 1966–67, pp. 163–67.

(235) Jenkins, J. S., "Motive and Intention." *PQ* Vol. 15, 1965, pp. 155–64.

(236) ———, "Dr. Peters' Motives." *M* LXXV, 1966, pp. 248–54.

(237) Joske, W. D., "Behaviorism as a Scientific Theory." *PPR* XXII, 1961–62, pp. 61–68.

(238) Kaiser, D. N., "Philippa Foot and the Concepts of Law, Intention, and Accident." *M* LXXVIII, 1969, pp. 273–77.

(239) Kashap, P., "Can a Man Act Upon a Proposition Which He Believes to be False?" *A* XXII, 1961–62, pp. 31–36.

(240) Kaufman, A. S., "Moral Responsibility and the Use of 'Could Have'." *PQ* XII, 1962, pp. 120–28.

(241) ———, "Ability." *JP* LX, 1963, pp. 537–51. Reprinted in Brand, M. (ed.) [(55) above].

(242) ———, "Practical Decision." *M* LXXV, 1966, pp. 25–44.

(243) Kenny, A., "Intention and Purpose." *JP* LXIII, 1966, pp. 642–51.

(244) Kjaergaad, A., "Action and the Person: McMurray's *The Form of the Personal*." *Inquiry* Vol. 13, 1970, pp. 160–75.

(245) Kneale, W., "Intentionality and Intensionality." *SPAS* XLII, 1968, pp. 73–90.

(246) Kolnai, A., "Deliberation is of Ends." *PAS* LXII, 1961–62, pp. 195–218.

(247) Korner, S., "On the Concept of the Practicable." *PAS* LXVII, 1966–67, pp. 1–16.

(248) Kotarbinski, T., "Concept of Action." *JP* LVII, 1960, pp. 215–22.

(249) Lacey, A. R., "Freewill and Determinism." *PAS* LVIII, 1957–58, pp. 15–32.

(250) ——, "Men and Robots." *PQ* Vol. 10, 1960, pp. 61–72.

(251) Ladd, J., "Free Will and Voluntary Action." *PPR* XII, 1951–52, pp. 392–405.

(252) ——, "The Ethical Dimensions of the Concept of Action." *JP* LXII, 1965, pp. 633–45.

(253) Landesman, C., "Actions as Universals: An Inquiry into the Metaphysics of Action." *APQ* Vol. 6, 1969, pp. 247–52.

(254) Lehrer, K., "Ifs, Cans and Causes." *A* XX, 1959–60, pp. 122–24. Reprinted in Brand, M. (ed.) [(55) above].

(255) ——, "Cans and Conditionals: A Rejoinder." *A* XXII, 1961–62, pp. 23–24. Reprinted in Brand, M. (ed.) [(55) above].

(256) ——, "Decisions and Causes." *PR* LXXII, 1963, pp. 224–27.

(257) ——, "'Could' and Determinism." *A* XIV, 1963–64, pp. 159–60.

(258) ——, "Cans Without Ifs." *A* XXIX, 1968–69, pp. 29–32.

(259) ——, "Neglecting to Do What One Can: A Reply." *M* LXXVIII, 1969, pp. 121–23.

(260) Lehrer, K. and Taylor, R., "Time, Truth and Modalities." *M* LXXV, 1965, pp. 390–98.

(261) Levi, I. and Morgenbesser, S., "Belief and Disposition." *APQ* Vol. 1, 1964, pp. 221–32.

(262) Levison, A. B. and Thalberg, I., "Essential and Causal Explanations of Action." *M* LXXVIII, 1969, pp. 91–101.

(263) Lloyd Thomas, D. A., "Consequences." *A* XVIII, 1967–68, pp. 133–41.

(264) Locke, D., "Ifs and Cans Revisited." *P* XXXVII, 1962, pp. 245–56.

(265) ——, "Intention and Intentional Action." In *The Business of Reason,* edited by S. Coval and J. J. McIntosh. Routledge & Kegan Paul, 1969.

(266) Lycan, W. G., "On 'Intentionality' and the Psychological." *APQ* Vol. 6, 1969, pp. 305–11.

(267) Mabbott, J. D., "Reason and Desire." *P* XXVIII, 1953, pp. 113–23.

(268) Mace, C. A., "Some Implications of Analytical Behaviorism." *PAS* XCIX, 1948–49, pp. 1–16.

(269) MacIntyre, A., "Purpose and Intelligent Action." *SPAS* XXXIV, 1960, pp. 79–96.

(270) ——, "A Mistake About Causality in Social Science." In *Philosophy, Politics and Society,* second series, edited by P. Laslett and W. G. Runciman. Blackwell, 1964, pp. 48–70.

(271) ——, "Pleasure as a Reason for Acting." *Monist* Vol. 49, 1965, pp. 215–33.

(272) ——, "The Antecedents of Action." Chapter 9 in *British Analytic Philosophy,* edited by B. Williams and A. Montefiore. Routledge & Kegan Paul, 1966, pp. 205–25.

(273) ——, "The Idea of a Social Science." *SPAS* XLI, 1967, pp. 95–114.

(274) Macklin, R., "Action, Causality and Teleology." *BJPS* Vol. 19, 1968–69, pp. 301–16.

(275) Madell, G., "Action and Causal Explanation." *M* LXXVI, 1967, pp. 34–48.

(276) Malcolm, N., "Explaining Behavior." *PR* LXXVI, 1967, pp. 97–104.

(277) ——, "The Conceivability of Mechanism." *PR* LXXVII, 1968, pp. 45–72.

(278) Mannison, D. S., "My Motive and Its Reasons." *M* LXXIII, 1964, pp. 423–29.

(279) ——, "Doing Something on Purpose but Not Intentionally." *A* XXX, 1969–70, pp. 49–52.

(280) Manser, A. R., "Pleasure." *PAS* LXI, 1960–61, pp. 223–38.

(281) Margolis, J., "Danto on Basic Actions." *Inquiry* Vol. 13, 1970, pp. 104–8.

(282) Marshall, G. D., "Attention and Will." *PQ* Vol. 20, 1970, pp. 14–25.

(283) Mathews, G., "A Note on Inference as Action." *A* XVI, 1955–56, pp. 136–37.

(284) Matson, W. I., "On the Irrelevance of Free Will to Moral Responsibility and the Vacuity of the Latter." *M* LXV, 1956, pp. 489–97.

(285) McAdam, J. I., "Choosing Flippantly or Nonrational Choice." *A* XXV, 1964–65, pp. 132–36.

(286) McCall, S., "Ability as a Species of Possibility." In Brand, M. (ed.) [(55) above].

(287) McCracken, D., "Motives and Causes." *SPAS* XXVI, 1952.

(288) McGuiness, B. F., "I Know What I Want." *PAS* LVII, 1956–57, pp. 305–20.

(289) McLaughlin, R. N., "Human Action." *AJP* XLV, 1967, pp. 141–58.

(290) Meiland, J. W., "Are There Unintentional Actions?" *PR* LXXII, 1963, pp. 377–81.

(291) ———, "Motives and Ends." *PQ* Vol. 13, 1963, pp. 64–71.

(292) Melden, A. I., "Action." *PR* LXV, 1956, pp. 523–41. Reprinted in *Essays in Philosophical Psychology*, edited by D. F. Gustafson. Garden City, New York: Doubleday & Company, 1964.

(293) ———, "Willing." *PR* LXIX, 1960, pp. 475–84. Reprinted in White, A. R. (ed.) [(72) above].

(294) Milligan, D., "Philosophy and the Social Sciences." *PAS* LXIX, 1968–69, pp. 51–72.

(295) Mischel, T., "Psychology and Explanations of Human Behavior." *PPR* XXIII, 1962–63, pp. 578–94.

(296) Mish'alani, J. K., "Can Right Acts Be Voluntary?" *A* XX, 1959–60, pp. 67–72.

(297) Mundle, C. W. K., "Philosophical Behaviourism." In *Knowledge and Necessity, Royal Institute of Philosophy Lectures*, Vol. 3, 1968–69. New York: The Macmillan Company, 1970.

(298) Munk, A. W., "The Self as Agent and Spectator." *Monist* Vol. 49, 1965, pp. 262–72.

(299) Myers, G. E., "Motives and Wants." *M* LXXII, 1964, pp. 173–85.

(300) Nagel, E., "Mechanistic Explanation and Organismic Biology." *PPR* XI, 1950–51, pp. 327–38.

(301) Nelson, R. J., "Behaviorism is False." *JP* LXVI, 1969, pp. 417–52.

(302) Noble, C., "Charles Taylor on Teleological Explanation." *A* XXVII, 1966–67, pp. 96–103.

(303) Noble, D., "The Conceptualist View of Teleology." *A* XVIII, 1967–68, pp. 62–63.

(304) Nowell-Smith, P. H., "Free Will and Moral Responsibility." *M* LVII, 1948, pp. 45–61.

(305) ———, "Choosing, Deciding and Doing." *A* XVIII, 1957–58, pp. 63–69.

(306) ———, "Ifs and Cans." *Theoria* XXVI, 1960, pp. 85–101. Reprinted in *Symposium on J. L. Austin*, edited by K. T. Fann. Routledge & Kegan Paul, 1969.

(307) ———, "Purpose and Intelligent Action." *SPAS* XXXIV, 1960, pp. 97–112.

(308) O'Connor, D. J., "Possibility and Choice." *SPAS* XXXIV, 1960, pp. 1–24.

(309) ———, "Beliefs, Dispositions and Actions." *PAS* LXIX, 1968–69, pp. 1–16.

(310) O'Connor, J., "How Decisions are Predicted." *JP* LXIV, 1967, pp. 429–30.

(311) Ofstad, H., "Recent Work on the Freewill Problem." *APQ* Vol. 4, 1967, pp. 179–207.

(312) Olsen, C., "Knowledge of One's Own Intentional Actions." *PQ* Vol. 19, 1969, pp. 324–36.

(313) O'Shaughnessy, B., "Observation and the Will." *JP* LX, 1963, pp. 367–92.

(314) ———, "The Limits of the Will." *PR* LXV, 1956, pp. 443–90.

(315) Pahuus, M., "On Determinism and the Nature of Persons." *Danish Yearbook of Philosophy*, Vol. 3, 1966, pp. 82–88.

(316) Palmer, A., "Thinking and Performances." In *Knowledge and Necessity, Royal Institute of Philosophy Lectures*, Vol. 3, 1968–69, pp. 107–18. New York: The Macmillan Company, 1970.

(317) Pashman, J., "Raziel Abelson on 'Because I Want to.'" *M* LXXVII, 1968, p. 581.

(318) Passmore, J. A., "Intentions." *SPAS* XXIX, 1955, pp. 131–46.

(319) Pears, D., "Predicting and Deciding." *Pr.B.A.* L, 1964, pp. 193–227.

(320) Penelhum, T., "Doing, Desiring, and Making Happen." *JP* LXI, 1964, pp. 625–27.

(321) Perry, D. L., "Prediction, Explanation and Freedom." *Monist* Vol. 49, 1965, pp. 234–47.

(322) Peters, R. S., "Observationism in Psychology." *M* LX, 1951, pp. 43–61.

(323) ———, "Motives and Causes." *SPAS* XXVI, 1952, pp. 139–62.

(324) ———, "Motives and Motivation." *P* XXXI, 1956, pp. 117–30.

(325) ———, "More about Motives." *M* LXXVI, 1967, pp. 92–97.

(326) Peters, R. S. and Tajfel, H., "Hobbes and Hull, Metaphysicians of Behaviour." *BJPS* Vol. 8, 1957, pp. 36–40.

(327) Pitcher, G., "Hart on Action and Responsibility." *PR* LXIX, 1960, pp. 226–35.

(328) Place, U. T., "Is Consciousness a Brain Process?" *British Journal of Psychology*, XLV, 1954, pp. 44–50. Reprinted in *The Philosophy of Mind*,

edited by V. C. Chappell. Englewood Cliffs, New Jersey: Prentice-Hall, 1962.

(329) Potts, T. C., "States, Activities and Performances." *SPAS* XXXIX, 1965, pp. 65–84.

(330) Powell, B., "Uncharacteristic Actions." *M* LXVIII, 1959, pp. 492–509.

(331) Price, H. H., "Some Considerations about Belief." *PAS* XXXV, 1934–35, pp. 229–52.

(332) Prior, A. N., "Intentionality and Intensionality." *SPAS* XLII, 1968, pp. 91–106.

(333) Pucetti, R., "On Thinking Machines and Feeling Machines." *BJPS* Vol. 18, 1967–68, pp. 39–51.

(334) Putnam, H., "Brains and Behaviour." In *Analytical Philosophy*, second series, edited by R. J. Butler. Blackwell, 1965.

(335) ———, "Robots: Machines or Artificially Created Life?" *JP* LXI, 1964, pp. 668–91. Reprinted in *Philosophy of Mind*, edited by S. Hampshire. New York: Harper & Row, 1966.

(336) Rachels, J., "Wants, Reasons and Justifications." *PQ* Vol. 18, 1968, pp. 299–309.

(337) Ranken, N. L., "The 'Unmoved' Agent and the Ground of Responsibility." *JP* LXIV, 1967, pp. 403–8.

(338) Rankin, K. W., "Causal Modalities and Alternative Action." *PQ* Vol. 7, 1957, pp. 289–304.

(339) Rayfield, D., "Action." *Nous* Vol. 2, 1968, pp. 131–45.

(340) ———, "On Describing Actions." *Inquiry* Vol. 13, 1970, pp. 90–99.

(341) Rescher, N., "Values and the Explanation of Behaviour." *PQ* Vol. 17, 1967, pp. 130–36.

(342) ———, "On the Characterisation of Actions." In Rescher, N. (ed.) [(68) above]. Reprinted in Brand, M. (ed.) [(55) above].

(343) Richman, R. J., "Responsibility and the Causation of Actions." *APQ* Vol. 6, 1969, pp. 186–97.

(344) ———, "Reasons and Causes." *AJP* XLVII, 1969, pp. 42–50.

(345) Ritchie, A. M., "Agent and Act in Theory of Mind." *PAS* LII, 1951–52, pp. 1–22.

(346) Robinson, D. S., "Royce's Concept of Modes of Action." *PPR* XIV, 1953–54, pp. 553–59.

(347) Rorty, A. O., "Slaves and Machines." *A* XXII, 1961–62, pp. 118–20.

(348) ———, "Wants and Justifications." *JP* LXIII, 1966, pp. 765–72.

(349) Rosenblueth, A., Wiener, N., and Bigelow, J., "Behaviour, Purpose, and Teleology." *Philosophy of Science*, 1943, pp. 18–24.

(350) Roxbee Cox, J. W., "Can I Know Beforehand What I Am Going to Decide?" *PR* LXXII, 1963, pp. 88–92.

(351) Ryle, G., "Knowing How and Knowing That." *PAS* XLVI, 1945–46, pp. 1–16.

(352) Sachs, D., "A Few Morals about Acts." *PR* LXXV, 1966, pp. 91–98.

(353) Samek, R. A., "The Concepts of Act and Intention and Their Treatment in Jurisprudence." *AJP* XLI, 1963, pp. 198–216.

(354) Scarrow, D. S., "On an Analysis of 'Could Have.'" *A* XXII, 1962–63, pp. 118–20.

(355) Schneewind, J. B., "Responsibilities and Liability." *JP* LXII, 1965, pp. 649–50.

(356) Schuetz, A., "Choosing among Projects of Action." *PPR* XII, 1951–52, pp. 161–84.

(357) Searle, J. R., "Assertions and Aberrations." In *British Analytical Philosophy*, edited by B. Williams and A. Montefiore. Reprinted in *Symposium on J. L. Austin*, edited by K. T. Fann. Routledge & Kegan Paul, 1969, pp. 41–54.

(358) Sellars, R. S., "Levels of Causality: The Emergence of Guidance and Reason in Nature." *PPR* XX, 1959–60, pp. 1–7.

(359) Sesonske, A., "Performatives." *JP* LXII, 1965, pp. 459–68.

(360) Sher, G., "Reasons and Intentionality." *JP* LXVI, 1969, pp. 164–68.

(361) Shwayder, D. S., "Topics on the Bordergrounds of Action." *Inquiry*, Vol. 13, 1970, pp. 32–53.

(362) Sikora, R. I., "Unforeseeable Consequences." *A* XXIX, 1968–69, pp. 89–91.

(363) Silber, J., "Human Action and the Language of Volitions." *PAS* LXIV, 1963–64, pp. 199–220.

(364) Simon, M. A., "Could There Be a Conscious Automation?" *APQ* Vol. 6, 1969, pp. 71–78.

(365) Skinner, B. F., "Behaviorism at Fifty." In *Behaviorism and Phenomenology*, edited by T. W. Wann. Chicago: University of Chicago Press, 1964, pp. 79–97.

(366) Smart, J. J. C., "Professor Ziff on Robots." *A* XIX, 1958–59, pp. 117–19.

(367) ———, "Sensations and Brain Processes." *PR* LXVIII, 1959, pp. 141–56. Reprinted in *The Philosophy of Mind*, edited by V. C. Chappell. Englewood Cliffs, New Jersey: Prentice-Hall, 1962.

(368) ———, "Causality and Human Behavior." *SPAS* XXXVIII, 1964, pp. 143–48.

(369) Smart, N., "Robots Incorporated." *A* XIX, 1958–59, pp. 119–20.

(370) Squires, R., "Are Dispositions Causes?" *A* XXIX, 1968–69, pp. 45–47.

(371) Stevenson, C. L., "Ethical Judgements and Avoidability." *M* XLVII, 1938, pp. 45–57. Reprinted in Stevenson's *Facts and Values*. New Haven, Connecticut: Yale University Press, 1963, pp. 138–52.

(372) Stigen, A., "The Concept of a Human Action." *Inquiry* Vol. 13, 1970, pp. 1–31.

(373) Stocker, M., "How to Prevent Self-Prediction." *JP* LXV, 1968, pp. 475–77.

(374) Stoljar, S., "Ascriptive and Prescriptive Responsibility." *M* LXVIII, 1959, pp. 350–60.

(375) Stoutland, F., "Basic Actions and Causality." *JP* LXV, 1968, pp. 467–75.

(376) Strawson, P. F., "Intention and Convention in Speech Acts." *PR* LXXIII, 1964, pp. 439–60.

(377) Sutherland, N. S., "Motives as Explanations." *M* LXVIII, 1959, pp. 145–59.

(378) Swiggart, P., "Doing and Deciding to Do." *A* XXII, 1962–63, pp. 17–19.

(379) Taylor, C., "Teleological Explanation—a Reply to Denis Noble." *A* XXVII, 1966–67, pp. 141–43.

(380) ——, "Explaining Actions." *Inquiry* Vol. 13, 1970, pp. 54–89.

(381) Taylor, C. C. W., "Pleasure." *A* XXII, 1962–63, pp. 2–19.

(382) ——, "States, Activities and Performances." *SPAS* XXXIX, 1965, pp. 85–102.

(383) Taylor, P. W., "'Need' Statements." *A* XIX, 1958–59, pp. 106–11.

(384) Taylor, R., "The Problem of Future Contingencies." *PR* LXVI, 1957, pp. 1–28.

(385) ——, "I Can." *PR* LXIX, 1960, pp. 78–89.

(386) ——, "Mechanism and Purpose." *JP* LXII, 1965, pp. 657–58.

(387) ——, "Thought and Purpose." *Inquiry* Vol. 12, 1969, pp. 149–69.

(388) Teichman, J., "Mental Cause and Effect." *M* LXX, 1961, pp. 36–52.

(389) Thalberg, I., "Abilities and Ifs." *A* XXII, 1961–62, pp. 121–26.

(390) ——, "Intending the Impossible." *AJP* XL, 1962, pp. 49–56.

(391) ——, "Foreknowledge and Decision in Advance." *A* XXIV, 1963–64, pp. 49–53.

(392) ——, "Freedom of Action and Freedom of Will." *JP* LXI, 1964, pp. 405–15.

(393) ——, "Do We Cause Our Own Actions?" *A* XXVII, 1966–67, pp. 196–201.

(394) ——, "Austin on Abilities." In *Symposium on J. L. Austin,* edited by K. T. Fann. Routledge & Kegan Paul, 1969.

(395) Thalberg, I. and McCormich, S., "Trying." *Dialogue* 6, 1967, pp. 29–46.

(396) Thomas, G., "Abilities and Physiology." *JP* LXI, 1964, pp. 321–28.

(397) Thompson, D., "Can a Machine be Conscious?" *BJPS* Vol. 16, 1965–66, pp. 33–43.

(398) Urmson, J. O., "Motives and Causes." *SPAS* XXVI, 1952, pp. 179–94. Reprinted in White, A. R. (ed.) [(72) above].

(399) ——, "Criteria of Intensionality." *SPAS* XLII, 1968, pp. 107–22.

(400) Vendler, Z. "Effects, Results and Consequences." In *Analytical Philosophy,* edited by R. J. Butler, Blackwell, 1962, pp. 1–15.

(401) Vesey, G. N. A., "Volition." *P* XXXVI, 1961, pp. 352–65. Reprinted in *Essays in Philosophical Psychology,* edited by D. F. Gustafson. Garden City, New York: Doubleday & Company, 1964.

(402) Wallace, J. D., "Pleasure as an End of Action." *APQ* Vol. 3, 1966, pp. 312–16.

(403) Walsh, J. J., "Remarks on *Thought and Action.*" *JP* LX, 1963, pp. 57–65.

(404) Walton, K. A., "Rational Action." *M* LXXVI, 1967, pp. 537–47.

(405) Watkins, J. W. N., "Decision and Belief." In *Decision Making,* edited by R. J. Audley. B.B.C. Publications, 1967.

(406) Wheatley, J. M. O., "Wishing and Hoping." *A* XVIII, 1957–58, pp. 121–31.

(407) ——, "Hampshire on Human Freedom." *PQ* Vol. 12, 1962, pp. 248–60.

(408) White, A. R., "Good at." *SPAS* XXXII, 1958, pp. 195–206.
(409) ———, "Different Kinds of Need Concepts." *A* XX, 1959–60, pp. 112–16.
(410) ———, "Inclination." *A* XXI, 1960–61, pp. 40–42.
(411) ———, "Explaining Human Behavior" (Inaugural lecture). University of Hull Publications, 1962.
(412) ———, "The Notion of Interest." *PQ* Vol. 14, 1964, pp. 319–27.
(413) ———, "Mentioning the Unmentionable." *A* XXVII, 1967, pp. 113–18. Reprinted in *Symposium on J. L. Austin*, edited by K. T. Fann. Routledge & Kegan Paul, 1969.
(414) Whiteley, C. H., "Can." *A* XXII, 1962–63, pp. 91–93.
(415) ———, "Responsibility." *SPAS* XL, 1966, pp. 223–34.
(416) Wilkins, B. T., "The Thing to Do." *M* LXXXIV, 1965, pp. 89–91.
(417) Will, F. L., "Intention, Error and Responsibility." *JP* LXI, 1964, pp. 171–79.
(418) Wisdom, W. A., "On How Donnellan Knows What He Is Doing." *JP* LX, 1963, pp. 589–90.
(419) Yolton, J. W., "My Hand Goes Out to You." *P* XLI, 1966, pp. 140–52.
(420) ———, "Agent Causality." *APQ* Vol. 3, 1966, pp. 14–26.
(421) Ziff, P., "About Behaviorism." *A* XVIII, 1957–58, pp. 132–36.
(422) ———, "The feelings of robots." *A* XIX, 1958–59, pp. 64–68.

INDEX